COPPER CHEF

Eric Theiss

First Edition

Published by Tristar Products, Inc.

Printed in China.

CCCB_COOKBOOK_TP_ENG_V1_160801

Acknowledgements

This project involved several key people without whom it would not have been possible. I'd like to thank Claire Winslow for her endless testing and tweaking of recipes, and Lynda Gentile for driving tough deadlines in the nicest way. I want to thank Matt Wagemann for his fantastic photography. I'd also like to thank Kris "Chez" Amerine for his culinary wisdom and comedic contributions along the way, which always help to make a project more fun. As always, thank you to Meredith Laurence, "The Blue Jean Chef," who never tires of having my back whenever I need her. I am very grateful to Keith Mirchandani and Josef Lavi for giving me this great opportunity.

I want to thank my wife, Jesse, for keeping our "life" in order while I focused on this project (and Cameron and Max for making that nearly impossible) and my mom, Arlene, who raised me to appreciate good food and taught me to always cook with love.

Eric Theiss

Table of Contents

Acknowledgements.....................................3

Table of Contents 4

About the Author.....................................9

Copper Chef Q & A 10

Why Copper Chef? 11

Finishing Touches.................................12

Cooking Temperature Chart 13

Equivalent Chart.................................14

Word on the Street 15

Everyone's Deep-Fried Favorites

Onion Rings.................................18

Fried Zucchini Sticks.................................19

Sweet Potato Fries 21

Garlic Truffle Fries 22

Corn Fritters.................................25

Vegetable Tempura 26

Coconut Shrimp.................................29

Bang Bang Chicken 30

Chicken Tenders.................................33

Spring Rolls 34

Sweet Chili Glazed Chicken Wings.....................36

Caribbean Jerk Chicken Wings 38

Parmesan Garlic Wings 39

Monte Cristo Americano 40

Country-Fried Steak.................................41

Fried Chicken 43

Chicken Milanese
with Arugula and Fennel Salad.........................44

Indulge! Deep-Fried Desserts

Fried Chocolate Cream-Filled Cookies.............48

Fried Brownies.................................50

Glazed Doughnuts 51

Pumpkin Doughnuts.................................52

Apple Fritters 53

Zeppole.................................55

Mouthwatering Oven-Roasted Recipes

Mom's Meatloaf.................................58

Roast Prime Rib of Beef.................................61

Spicy Cowboy Steak 62

Roast Beef 65

Classic Roasted Chicken 66

Spicy Brick Chicken.................................67

Orange Brine Turkey Breast.................................69

Miso-Glazed Salmon 70

BBQ Baby Back Ribs 73

Jerk Ribs.................................74

Roasted Pork Loin.................................75

Bacon-Wrapped Roast Pork 77

Rosemary Rack of Lamb 78

Simply Sautéed

Philly Cheesesteak 82

Shrimp and Saffron Risotto 84

Chicken Alfredo 85

Texas Smokehouse Stuffed Burger 86

Chicken Paprikash 88

Chicken Breasts with Tomato Tapenade 90

Cuban Pork Asado with Black Bean Relish 91

Pan-Seared Herb Pork Chops
with Apple Slaw 93

Spicy Mussels 95

Summer Clams 96

Pork Marsala
with Mushrooms and Spinach 98

Crab Cakes 99

Pan-Seared Scallops Over Greens 100

Hot and Sweet Sausage and Peppers 103

Tilapia Francese 104

Pan-Seared Tuna
with Mango Pineapple Salsa 106

Salmon Burgers 108

Flounder in Saffron Tomato Broth 109

Prosciutto-Wrapped Cod
with Edamame Salad 110

Fusilli and Clams 111

Linguini Carbonara 112

Penne alla Vodka 115

Eric's Braised Creations

Meatballs and Sunday Gravy 118

Swedish Meatballs 121

Veal and Peppers 122

Coq Au Vin 123

Chicken Cacciatore 124

Chicken and Dumplings 125

Green Chile Pork 126

Braised Pork Shoulder
with Browned Sauerkraut 127

Pork Osso Buco 129

Braised Pork Shoulder 130

Beef Stew 131

Pork Braciole 133

Braised Lamb Shanks 134

Lamb Stew 136

Wiener Schnitzel
with Braised Red Cabbage 137

Savory Baked Meals

Shepherd's Pie 140

Beef Enchiladas 141

Chicken Parm 142

Chicken Pot Pie 143

Sausage Frittata 144

Stuffed Pork Medallions 145

Pineapple-Glazed Ham 147

Teriyaki Pork Tenderloins 148

Quiche Lorraine 149

Giant Frittata 150

Bleu Cheese Stuffed Mushrooms 153

Lime Cilantro Seafood Bake........................... 154

Eggplant Parmesan 155

Au Gratin Potatoes 156

Spaghetti Pie.. 159

Sweet Potatoes with Marshmallows 160

Baked Ziti 161

Noodle Kugel 162

Vegetable Lasagna 163

Decadent Baked Desserts

Blueberry Breakfast Cake
with Crumb Topping 166

Coffee Cake... 168

Black Forest Cake.................................... 169

Coconut Cake....................................... 171

Peanut Butter Brownies 172

Cornbread.. 174

Baklava 175

Pumpkin Cake 176

Banana Nut Bread................................... 177

Sticky Buns 178

Cheesecake Brownies 179

Easy Stir-Fried Favorites

Spicy Asian Beef Wraps.............................. 183

Steak and Soba Noodles 184

Pepper Steak.. 187

Pork Fried Rice...................................... 188

Asparagus, Bacon and Spinach....................... 191

Shrimp and Asparagus............................... 192

Mongolian Beef 194

Vegetable Fried Rice................................. 195

Vegetable Lo Mein................................... 196

Home-Cooked Soups & Chilies

Cream of Mushroom 200

White Bean 201

Split Pea..202

Roasted Cauliflower Soup
with Brown Butter 203

Thai Coconut Chicken Soup 204

New England Clam Chowder 205

Shrimp Gumbo 207

Shrimp Bisque......................................208

Eric's Beef Chili.....................................209

Seafood Bouillabaisse 210

Classic Beef Barley..................................212

Tortilla Soup..213

Pozole Guerrero 214

Eric's French Quarter Chili.............................215

Super Easy Turkey Chili.............................217

Light & Healthy Steamed Selections

Cheese and Onion Pierogies 220

Greek Wonton Pot Stickers.............................222

Chicken and Scallion Pot Stickers 223

Pesto-Stuffed Flounder 224

New England Clam Bake 225

Halibut with Dijon and Tomato Drizzle 227

Herb-Steamed Shrimp 228

Steamed Salmon
with Leeks and Asparagus.............................229

Whole Thai Steamed Snapper.............................230

Herb-Steamed Potatoes.............................232

Steamed Snow Crab Legs.............................233

Index 234

About the Author

Eric Theiss' culinary savoir-faire started in northern New Jersey as a child when his Italian mother, on a hunch, borrowed from the public library his first cookbook at age 6. His mother was right, and Eric began a life of culinary work. As a young adult, he continued to fuel his passion for food and fine dining. During his early twenties, his love of food and wine manifested itself in working long nights in NJ restaurants, including his favorite kitchen of all at The Culinary Renaissance. There, acclaimed chef Frank Falcinelli[1] exposed Eric to a level of culinary passion that inspired him to strive for excellence. In 1997, he took a leap of faith and opened his own fine dining restaurant and bar called Meritage in West Chester, PA, where he enjoyed rave reviews from prominent Philadelphia food critics. Here, his dream of owning and operating a fine dining establishment was fully realized.

A few years later, utilizing his inventive and creative flair, Eric moved on to the culinary broadcast world, working in product development not only for QVC's proprietary kitchenware lines but also for celebrity lines (Paula Deen, Emeril, Rocco DiSpirito, Rachael Ray) as well as his own personal line of cool kitchen tools and cookware, Walah! Eric has been a popular regular TV Chef presenter for over 10 years on QVC's live shows for his own brands as well as a variety of well-known national kitchen names. Beyond that, Eric owns and operates a company that brokers into QVC many new and innovative products. His most recent business venture, a successful new publishing company (also named Walah!), publishes cookbooks and pamphlets distributed nationwide.

Paramount to his career thus far, Eric currently hosts, among others, the incredibly successful, award-winning long-form infomercial featuring the Power Pressure Cooker XL, which has sold over a million units and achieved a TOP 5 status. Eric wrote this cookbook to complement the Power Pressure Cooker infomercial, answering the calls of millions of customers for delicious, easy recipes.

Eric currently resides near the live studios at QVC in PA along with his wife, Jessica, and his two sons, Cameron and Maxwell.

---

[1] Owner of NY Restaurants Frankies 457, Frankies Sputino, Prime Meats and Café Pedlar.

Copper Chef Q & A

Q: What makes the Copper Chef™ pan so extraordinary?

A: Copper Chef sets the gold standard in today's busy kitchens. Every pan is constructed with advanced Cerami-Tech Nonstick Technology. Copper Chef is heatproof up to 850° F with a unique square shape for 25% more cooking space. You get versatility and the convenience of professional, nonstick cooking in an attractive, classic copper style. To view the complete collection of our best-selling nonstick pans, visit copperchefcollections.com.

Q: Can I use cooking sprays in the Copper Chef™?

A: Although you can use cooking sprays, they can sometimes decrease the effectiveness of the nonstick coating. Eric recommends real, 100% natural oils, such as olive oil for sautéeing, and canola or peanut oil for frying.

Q: What is the bottom of the Copper Chef™ pan made of?

A: The bottom induction plate is made of stainless steel, which is then pressed into the aluminum.

Q: Can you cook on an open fire with the Copper Chef™ pan?

A: Although the pan can be used on an open fire, it is designed for kitchen use.

Q: How do I clean my Copper Chef™ pan?

A: Clean your Copper Chef™ pan with mild soap and water and a soft, non-metal scrubber.

Q: Does the handle on the Copper Chef™ pan get hot?

A: The handle is hollow, making it cooler than solid-core handles. Be sure to use a pot holder, as the handle can get hot on the stovetop and when in the oven.

Q: Is the Copper Chef™ pan oven-safe?

A: Yes, though you should always remember to use pot holders or an oven mitt when removing the pan from the oven.

Q: Is the glass lid oven-safe?

A: The glass lid is oven-safe up to 400° F. If the pan has been in the oven or on a stovetop, you should always remember to use pot holders or an oven mitt when removing the lid. Caution: the glass lid should never be put on or near an open flame or under the broiler.

Q: What kind of cooking utensils should I use with the Copper Chef™ pan?

A: Non-metallic utensils made of plastic, silicone, wood, or bamboo should be used.

Q: Is the Copper Chef™ pan dishwasher safe?

A: Yes!

Why Copper Chef?

Copper Chef's Conception

One of the things my customers always seem to want is to pare down the amount of pots and pans they have in their kitchen cabinets. I wanted to bring customers an "all around square pan" that seriously replaces most other pots and pans in the kitchen. Having worked in the cookware industry for nearly 20 years, I know a lot about cookware fabrication and about different types of nonstick. Most people want a pan that is not too heavy, free from harmful chemicals, nonstick for easy clean-up, and can stand up to the rigors of the hot oven. Copper Chef is the culmination of all of the above! Its lightweight construction is easy on the wrists. Copper Chef is designed with a durable and technologically advanced ceramic nonstick that lasts for years, even when it's being used as a workhorse on the stovetop and in the oven. We even outfitted Copper Chef with an induction plate so that it also works on induction stovetops.

It's Hip to Be Square

I wanted Copper Chef to be deep and square in shape instead of round because you can fit so much more food into a deep, square pan. Where you might only fit three chicken breasts or pork chops, for instance, in a round pan, you can fit a full four (or more) in a square-shaped pan of the same capacity. This makes it easier and more efficient to cook for your entire family all at once.

Copper Chef's Many Talents

I organized this cookbook into chapters that reflect all of the ways Copper Chef can be a workhorse in your kitchen. It's a sauté pan, a deep-fryer, a steamer, a baker, a slow cooker, a roaster, and so much more. It comes with a fry basket for making your favorite deep-fried foods like fried chicken and French fries, and also acts as a pasta cooker and strainer, eliminating the need for a separate colander. You also get the benefits of the steamer tray that allows you to make lighter and healthier dishes as well. You can oven-roast in Copper Chef because it goes into the oven up to 500° F and the capacity is huge. (You can fit up to a 5 lb. roast in Copper Chef!) Getting rid of some of the other less versatile pans you have in your kitchen cabinets simply increases your kitchen storage space and also simplifies your culinary life!

Finishing Touches
Thickening and Finishing Your Recipes

When I want a thicker result for my gravy, sauce or stew, there are many different ways to achieve that. Here are some of the ways I do this:

ROUX — This is the most classic way to thicken sauces, soups, stews, etc. A roux is an equal mixture of wheat flour and fat (traditionally butter). The butter is melted in a small pot and then the flour is added. The mixture is stirred until the flour is well incorporated and the desired color has been achieved, about 2-3 minutes, usually. The end result is a thickening agent to be added to your sauce, gravy, or stew. If you use 1 oz. (2 tbsp.) of flour and 1 oz. (2 tbsp.) of butter, for instance, you could add that to a volume 8 times larger (in this case, 1 cup of your gravy or sauce) and it would be correctly proportioned as a thickening agent.

SLURRY — Sometimes a slurry is preferable because you use ½ the amount of cornstarch to thicken that you would of flour. Also, it is gluten-free and usually lump-free. To make a "slurry," mix one tablespoon of cornstarch with ½ cup of cold water. Whisk until blended well and thickened, then add it to your sauce or gravy.

INSTANT POTATO FLAKES — I don't remember how I found out about this trick, but I feel it is the easiest of all thickening methods. Simply add a ¼ cup of instant potato flakes to your sauce, gravy or stew, and stir. After a couple of minutes, if you want an even thicker result, simply sprinkle in more flakes until desired thickness is achieved. This does not interfere with the flavor of your meal.

SIMMERING — By simply lowering the stovetop heat to low, you can reduce your sauce or gravy using evaporation. It's important to keep an eye on your sauce or gravy while it is simmering to ensure that you don't over-thicken it. Remember to stir occasionally.

BUTTER — In a lot of cases, I like to add a tablespoon or two of butter (depending on the volume of the sauce/gravy) at the end of the cooking process. This adds a really nice shimmer and "mouth feel" to the sauce or gravy you've cooked.

TOMATO PASTE — A staple that I use a lot in my dishes is tomato paste. If tomato is a flavor profile that you are adding to your dish, tomato paste is a great way to do that and it adds a thickness and richness to the final result. The paste will really shine through if you choose to reduce the sauce by simmering.

DRIED HERBS — Just as in traditional cooking, you can use dried herbs during the cooking process but should not use them to "finish" the dish.

FRESH HERBS — Wherever possible, I always recommend finishing the dishes you cook with chopped fresh herbs. This adds brightness and an extra layer of flavor at the end. Most of the time, fresh herbs won't stand up to any lengthy cooking for that matter. An exception to this would be what is referred to as a "bouquet garni," which is when you bundle fresh herbs, tie them together with twine, and add to the pot before cooking. An example of a typical bouquet would consist of parsley, basil, rosemary, bay leaf, and thyme. This bouquet is removed prior to serving the food. Experiment with other herbs as you wish for stocks, soups, and stews.

Cooking Temperature Chart

Safe steps in food handling, cooking, and storage are essential in preventing foodborne illness. You can't see, smell, or taste harmful bacteria that may cause illness. In every step of food preparation, follow the four guidelines to help keep food safe:

Clean—Wash hands and surfaces often.

Separate—Separate raw meat from other foods.

Cook—Cook to the right temperature.

Chill—Refrigerate food promptly.

Cook all food to these minimum internal temperatures as measured with a food thermometer before removing food from the heat source. Let rest for a minimum of 10 minutes before serving, unless indicated otherwise.

Doneness	Eric's Recommended Serving Temperature	USDA Recommended Serving Temperature
Beef, Lamb, Pork, Veal Steaks, Chops & Roasts		
Rare	125° F (52° C)	*
Medium-rare	130° F (54° C)	*
Medium	135° F (57° C)	*Minimum Internal Temperature & Rest Time:
Medium-well	150° F (65° C)	145° F (63° C) and allow to rest for at least
Well-done	over 150° F (over 65° C)	3 minutes
Ground Meats, Burgers, Meat Loaf & Sausages, Except Poultry		
Recommended	160° F (71° C)	*Minimum Internal Temperature: 160° F (71° C)
Burgers (Beef)		
Recommended	140° F (60° C)	*160° F (71° C)
Pork Ribs, Pork Shoulders		
Tender and Juicy	180-190° F (82-88° C)	*
Pre-cooked Ham		
Recommended	140° F (60° C)	*Reheat cooked hams packaged in USDA-inspected plants to 140° F (60° C); all others to 165° F (74° C)
Turkey & Chicken, Whole or Ground		
Recommended	165° F (74° C)	*Minimum Internal Temperature: 165° F (74° C)
Fish		
Rare	125° F (52° C)	*
Medium	135° F (57° C)	*
Well-done	145° F (63° C)	*Minimum Internal Temperature: 145° F (62.8° C)
Unpasteurized Eggs		
Recommended	160° F (71° C)	*Minimum Internal Temperature: 160° F (71° C)

*Consuming raw or undercooked meats, poultry, seafood, shellfish, or eggs may increase your risk of foodborne illness.
*Source: http://fsis.usda.gov/

Equivalent Chart

The charts below use standard U.S. Government guidelines. The charts offer equivalents for United States, metric, and Imperial (U.K.) measures. All conversions are approximate and most have been rounded up or down to the nearest whole number.[1]

Examples below:
1 teaspoon = 4.929 millimeters - rounded up to 5 millimeters
1 ounce = 28.349 grams - rounded to 28 grams

Dry/Weight Measurements

		Ounces
1/6 teaspoon	a dash	
1/8 teaspoon or less	a pinch or 6 drops	
1/4 teaspoon	15 drops	
1/2 teaspoon	30 drops	
1 teaspoon	1/3 tablespoon	1/6 ounce
3 teaspoon	1 tablespoon	1/2 ounce
1 tablespoon	3 teaspoons	1/2 ounce
2 tablespoons	1/8 cup	1 ounce
4 tablespoons	1/4 cup	2 ounces
5 tablespoons plus 1 tablespoons	1/3 cup	2.6 ounces
8 tablespoons	1/2 cup	4 ounces
10 tablespoons plus 2 teaspoons	2/3 cup	5.2 ounces
12 tablespoons	3/4 cup	6 ounces
16 tablespoons	1 cup	8 ounces
32 tablespoons	2 cups	16 ounces
64 tablespoons	4 cups or 1 quart	32 ounces

Liquid or Volume Measurements

	Pint	Quart	Gallon	U.S. Fluid Ounce	U.S. Tablespoon
jigger or measure	-	-	-	1.5	3
1 cup	1/2	-	-	8	16
2 cups	1	-	-	16	32
4 cups	2	1	1/4	32	64

[1] http://whatscookingamerica.net/Q-A/equiv.htm

Word on the Street

What some of my customers are saying...

"*I am so delighted with my Copper Chef Cookware. I have tried several recipes and have enjoyed all of them. My roast chicken was so succulent and my pot roast so tender and flavorful. I am so happy with this product that I am going to throw out all my other cookware and replace it with Copper Chef. I am also going to purchase some for family and friends. Oh, and did I mention the ease of clean-up? Awesome!!!*" Diane Calderon

"*When I first saw it on TV I thought it was a trick, but I was wrong. My family and I think this is the best pan I have ever used, no matter what I cook nothing sticks to it. It's wonderful.*" Bill Dennis

"*All I can say is...WOW! We are so enjoying our Copper Chef cooking pans and utensils. Everything we have made in the pans browns up so nicely and tastes so good. Pork chops are yummy, omelettes puff up beautifully, veggies taste like they have been grilled. Best of all, everything prepared without the addition of any unnecessary fats makes a much healthier meal. Thank you for making our lives easier and healthier! Again, WOW! I drop it right in the dishwasher or run under hot water and everything rinses right out! We are so grateful to the makers of the Copper Chef.....we love, love, love you and your product!*" Donna Elsaesser

"*I just want to say, I love my square pans! They boil water faster than my stainless steel set and they don't burn my food. My soup comes out perfect and in so much less time. I do let it simmer for a while anyway. My husband wants to know if you are making a 3 cup square saucepan? He loves it too but won't let me get rid of my stainless steel until I can make some 'square' gravy too!*" Becky Rebecca Reynolds

"*This is absolutely a great product! I do not usually buy from infomercials, but I had to try it after witnessing how incredible it looked. And when I tried it both on the stovetop and now the oven, it really does what it advertised it does! Thank you for making it so easy. I am not good at cooking but at least this gives me a shot at making good meals!*" Maria Debora Ribaya

"*Love this pan! It's large enough for a big meal, (I have chili going now) and the sides are high enough that frying chicken won't spatter all over my stovetop. It looks wonderful and clean-up is a breeze. I made pasta & sauce in it, using the basket to cook the pasta, and while it drained I made the sauce. I'm proud to have this wonderful pan hanging in my kitchen for all to see!*" Sherry Bowman

Everyone's
Deep-Fried Favorites

Onion Rings

Fried Zucchini Sticks

Sweet Potato Fries

Garlic Truffle Fries

Corn Fritters

Vegetable Tempura

Coconut Shrimp

Bang Bang Chicken

Chicken Tenders

Spring Rolls

Sweet Chili Glazed Chicken Wings

Caribbean Jerk Chicken Wings

Parmesan Garlic Wings

Monte Cristo Americano

Country-Fried Steak

Fried Chicken

**Chicken Milanese
with Arugula and Fennel Salad**

People tell me how much they love to fry food, but the reason that they stop short is because they have to drag out the giant deep fryer from their garage or basement where they store it. It always has to be cleaned at that point; so, instead of having some fun and frying up some deliciousness, the zt just collects dust. We designed Copper Chef to come complete with all of the accessories you need, including a fry basket. Thanks to the depth of the pan, you can easily fry just about any food you can think of using the Copper Chef pan! It's fun to get creative—try frying something you never would have fried before!

Ingredients

1 onion, yellow, large, sliced in ½" rings

1 cup buttermilk, whole

1 cup flour, all-purpose

1 cup panko breadcrumbs

2 tbsp. sea salt

2 tsp. ground black pepper

1 tsp. onion powder

1 tsp. dry mustard

2 qt. canola oil

Onion Rings

Directions

1. Separate the onion rings. Place them into the buttermilk and set aside.

2. Mix the flour, panko breadcrumbs, and the seasonings in a large bowl.

3. Place the Copper Chef on medium heat and fill halfway with canola oil. Heat to 365° F.

4. Dip onion rings into the flour/panko breadcrumb mixture, being sure to cover well. Use tongs to carefully place rings into the hot oil. Cook until lightly golden.

5. Serve.

Eric's Tip: I love to take the leftover rings and use them as egg cups. Just heat Copper Chef on medium with the rings, add a little olive oil, then crack an egg in the middle!

SERVES 4-6

Ingredients

2 eggs

1 cup milk

1 cup flour, all purpose

½ tsp. sea salt

½ tsp. ground black pepper

2 tbsp. Parmesan cheese, grated

1 tsp. garlic powder

3 zucchini, cut into fries

2 qt. canola oil, for frying

Dipping Sauce:

1 cup plain yogurt

1 tsp. fresh horseradish

1 tbsp. orange zest

1 small onion, peeled and chopped small

½ tsp. ground black pepper

½ tsp. sea salt

Fried Zucchini Sticks

Directions

1. Mix the eggs and milk together in a medium bowl. Add the flour, seasoning, Parmesan cheese, and garlic powder to the egg mixture. Mix well.

2. Place the Copper Chef on medium heat and fill halfway with canola. Heat to 365° F.

3. Carefully lower the fry basket into the pan. Caution: the oil will be HOT!

4. Dip the zucchini fries into the batter and shake off excess batter. Carefully place into the hot oil.

5. Carefully shake the basket to make sure they don't stick together.

6. Cook until golden.

7. In a bowl, mix the dipping sauce ingredients. Stir well and serve.

Eric's Tip: Using these in a traditional French fry recipe such as Poutine is a fantastic flip!

Ingredients

2-4 sweet potatoes, peeled and cut into fries

1 cup cornstarch

1 pack Italian dressing seasoning

1 tbsp. brown sugar

1 tsp. ground black pepper

1 tsp. salt

2 qt. canola oil, for frying

Sweet Potato Fries

Directions

1. Soak the cut fries in water for 10 minutes. Drain.

2. Dredge the fries in the cornstarch (you may need more depending on the size of your potatoes).

3. Place the Copper Chef on medium-high heat and fill with canola oil halfway. Heat to 365° F.

4. Carefully place the fry basket into the pan. Caution: the oil will be HOT. In batches, add the fries. Cook for 2 or 3 minutes to blanch, then pull them up to drain. For best results, never overfill the fry basket.

5. Drop them again into the hot oil and cook until lightly golden.

6. Shake off excess oil.

7. In a large bowl, mix brown sugar, black pepper, salt and Italian seasoning.

8. Toss the fries to season.

Eric's Tip: Think outside of the box for some interesting dips like spicy sriracha ketchup, salsa ranch dip, or honey maple mustard.

Ingredients

3 Idaho potatoes, peeled & cut into French fries

1 bowl ice water

1 tbsp. granulated garlic

3 tbsp. truffle oil

1 tbsp. sea salt

1 tsp. ground black pepper

2 qt. canola oil

Garlic Truffle Fries

Directions

1. Place cut potatoes into the bowl of ice water. Place in refrigerator for at least an hour.

2. Place the Copper Chef on medium-high heat and fill halfway with canola oil. Heat the oil to 365° F.

3. Carefully place the fry basket into the Copper Chef.

4. Remove the fries from the water and dry. Place a handful of fries in the basket at a time. Slowly and carefully drop the fries into the oil and cook for 3 minutes to blanch them. Remove the fries and set aside until all the fries are blanched.

5. Place a handful of the blanched fries back into the basket to cook until golden.

6. Before serving, toss the cooked fries with the granulated garlic, truffle oil, sea salt, and black pepper.

Eric's Tip: One of my absolute favorite things in this world is eating these fries topped with a homemade Hollandaise sauce. A local restaurant I go to lists them on the menu as "Sexy Fries."

Ingredients

2 ears corn, removed from cob

2 scallions, cleaned and chopped

¼ green pepper, diced

1 egg

¼ cup milk

⅓ cup flour

½ tsp. sea salt

1 tsp. sugar

½ tsp. cumin

1 tsp. baking powder

½ tsp. cayenne pepper

2 qt. canola oil

Corn Fritters

Directions

1. Place the Copper Chef on medium-high heat. Fill halfway with canola oil.

2. Heat the oil to 365° F. Carefully place the fry basket into the Copper Chef.

3. In a medium bowl, add the corn, scallions, peppers, egg, and milk. Mix well.

4. Add the rest of the ingredients. Mix well.

5. Lower the fry basket into the oil. Spoon in the batter 1 tablespoon at a time.

6. Cook until lightly golden. Remove and serve.

Eric's Tip: I love turning up the heat by adding diced jalapeño to the batter, and then serving with Thai sweet chili sauce.

Ingredients

1 cup water

3 egg whites, large

1½ cups flour, all purpose

6 mushrooms, white

1 sweet potato, peeled and sliced

10 asparagus stalks

6 carrots, baby

2 qt. canola oil, for frying

Dipping Sauce:

¼ cup rice vinegar

¼ cup soy sauce

2 tbsp. sesame oil

1 tbsp. orange marmalade

2 tbsp. ginger, peeled

2 cloves garlic, peeled

1 small onion, peeled and quartered

toasted sesame seeds, garnish for sauce

Vegetable Tempura

Directions

1. In a large bowl, make the batter by mixing water, egg whites, and flour together.

2. Place the Copper Chef on medium heat and fill with canola oil halfway. Heat oil to 365° F.

3. Carefully place the fry basket into the Copper Chef pan. Caution: the oil will be HOT!

4. Dip the vegetables into the batter one at a time. Shake off excess batter before dropping each carefully into the oil.

5. Repeat until all are cooked.

6. Shake off excess oil.

7. To make the dipping sauce, place all ingredients in the blender except onions and garlic. Blend, then add onions and garlic. Pulse a few times until the onion and garlic are chopped. Serve with toasted sesame seeds.

Eric's Tip: Using ginger ale instead of water will lighten the batter and give a nice, sweet flavor.

Ingredients

2 lb. large shrimp, peeled and deveined

2 cups egg whites, beaten

½ cup water

1 cup cornstarch

3 cups shredded coconut

1 cup panko breadcrumbs

2 qt. canola oil

Dipping Sauce:

¼ cup orange marmalade

2 tbsp. sweet chili sauce

1 tbsp. soy sauce

2 tbsp. rice vinegar

2 scallions, chopped

Coconut Shrimp

Directions

1. Mix the egg whites and water together. Set aside.

2. Mix the shredded coconut and the panko breadcrumbs together in a flat pan or bowl. Set aside.

3. Dip the shrimp into the cornstarch, then into the egg white mixture, and finally into the coconut mixture.

4. Place the Copper Chef on medium-high heat. Fill halfway with canola oil. Heat the oil to 365° F.

5. Place the fry basket into the Copper Chef. Carefully drop the shrimp into the basket and cook until golden, about 4-5 minutes.

6. In a bowl, mix all the dipping sauce ingredients together. Serve.

Eric's Tip: Sometimes, I use fresh sea scallops for this recipe. You can put them on a skewer as "lollipops" for party hors d'oeuvres.

SERVES 4

Ingredients

½ cup milk

½ cup cornstarch

¼ cup flour

1 large egg

1 tbsp. hot sauce

1 tsp. sea salt

2 chicken breasts, trimmed and cut into 1" pieces

2 cups panko breadcrumbs

2 qt. canola oil

Sauce:

1 tbsp. olive oil

2 scallions, chopped

½ tsp. ginger, minced

1 clove garlic, peeled and minced

1 tbsp. red curry powder

1 cup coconut milk

½ cup chicken stock

Bang Bang Chicken

Directions

1. Place the Copper Chef on medium-high heat, then fill halfway with canola oil. Heat the oil to 365° F. Place the fry basket into the oil carefully.

2. In a bowl, mix together milk, flour, cornstarch, egg, hot sauce, and sea salt.

3. Dip the chicken into the batter, then into a bowl of panko breadcrumbs, and next into the oil.

4. In batches, cook until lightly golden, about 4-5 minutes. Never overfill the basket.

For the sauce:

5. Place the clean Copper Chef on medium heat and add the olive oil.

6. Sauté the scallions, ginger, and garlic for 2 minutes. Add the rest of the ingredients and cook for 4-5 minutes. Lower the heat and reduce the sauce by about a third.

7. Drizzle the sauce over the chicken before serving.

Eric's Tip: I love these in lettuce wraps with some fresh julienned vegetables.

SERVES 4

Ingredients

1 cup flour

3 eggs

¼ cup milk

1 ½ cups seasoned breadcrumbs

1 cup crushed crackers

1 lb. chicken tenders, trimmed

1 tsp. sea salt

1 tsp. ground black pepper

2 qt. canola oil

Chicken Tenders

Directions

1. Season chicken with sea salt and black pepper.

2. In a bowl, mix together the eggs and milk. Set aside.

3. In a flat pan or a bowl, add the flour. In another flat pan or bowl, add the breadcrumbs and crushed crackers. Mix together.

4. Dip the chicken into the flour, then the egg mix, and finally the breadcrumb mix.

5. Place the Copper Chef on medium heat. Fill halfway with canola oil. Heat the oil to 365° F.

6. Place the fry basket carefully into the Copper Chef.

7. Carefully drop the chicken into the pan and cook for about 7 or 8 minutes until golden.

8. Serve.

Eric's Tip: I love filling warm corn tortillas with chicken tenders, cheddar cheese, crispy bacon, and BBQ sauce to make delicious street tacos!

MAKES 20-25 ROLLS

Ingredients

3 tbsp. canola oil, to sear vegetables

3 cups savoy cabbage, shredded

1 tsp. sea salt

1 carrot, peeled and diced small

1 head savoy cabbage

15 shiitake mushrooms, stemmed and chopped

1 tsp. ginger root, peeled and minced

½ tsp. garlic cloves, peeled and minced

3 scallions, chopped

½ cup water chestnuts, chopped

1 egg yolk

2 tbsp. water

1 package spring roll wraps

2 qt. canola oil, for frying

Sauce:

¼ cup rice vinegar

¼ cup soy sauce

2 tbsp. sesame oil

1 tbsp. orange marmalade

2 tbsp. ginger, peeled

2 cloves garlic, peeled

1 small onion, peeled and quartered

Spring Rolls

Directions

1. Place the Copper Chef on high heat. Add half the canola oil and savoy cabbage. Sprinkle with salt and sear for about 4 minutes. Remove and set aside.

2. Add the rest of the oil and sear the carrot pieces and mushrooms for about 4 minutes. Add the scallions, garlic, and ginger. Cook for 2 minutes, then add to the savoy cabbage that has been set aside.

3. Add the chopped water chestnuts to the savoy cabbage. Mix well and let cool.

4. Make an egg wash with the yolk and water.

5. Place a spring roll wrap on the counter. Add some savoy cabbage filling, then brush the edges with the egg wash. Roll like a burrito. Repeat until finished.

6. Place the cleaned Copper Chef on medium heat. Once preheated, add canola oil until pan is half full and heated to 365° F.

7. Cook the spring rolls in the oil until golden.

8. For the dipping sauce, add all sauce ingredients, except garlic and onion, to a blender. Blend. Add the garlic and onion. Pulse until chopped.

9. Serve spring rolls with dipping sauce.

Eric's Tip: If you need to prepare these in advance, give the rolls a light sprinkling of cornstarch and wrap in parchment individually.

Sweet Chili Glazed Chicken Wings

Ingredients

2 dozen fresh chicken wings

1 cup sweet chili sauce

2 tbsp. rice vinegar

1 tbsp. soy sauce

2 qt. canola oil

Directions

1. Place the Copper Chef on medium-high heat. Fill halfway with canola oil. Heat to 365° F.

2. Place the fry basket into the Copper Chef. Add the wings in 3 batches. Cook for about 6 minutes or until golden and crispy.

3. In a bowl, make the sauce by mixing the rest of the ingredients. When the wings are done, toss them in the sauce until coated.

4. Remove wings from sauce before serving.

Eric's Tip: Instead of bleu cheese dressing for dipping, I prefer to take some creamy ranch and add the zest and juice of a lime for a little zing.

Caribbean Jerk Chicken Wings

Ingredients

2 dozen fresh wings

3 tbsp. honey

2 tbsp. brown sugar

2 cloves garlic, minced

½ tsp. allspice

½ tsp. cinnamon

½ roasted red pepper

1 sprig thyme

½ red onion

2 scotch bonnets, stemmed and seeded

2 tbsp. light soy sauce

1 tbsp. water

2 qt. canola oil

Directions

1. Place the Copper Chef on medium-high heat. Fill halfway with canola oil. Heat the oil to 360° F.

2. Carefully place the fry basket into the Copper Chef. Add the wings in 3 batches. Cook for about 6 minutes or until golden and crispy.

3. In a bowl, make the sauce by mixing the rest of the ingredients. When the wings are done, toss them in the sauce until coated.

4. Remove the cooked wings from the sauce before serving.

Eric's Tip: This sauce isn't just for wings! I love to marinate chicken thighs in the jerk sauce and then grill them up. If you are looking for something lighter, try it with skinless chicken breasts.

Ingredients

2 dozen fresh wings

1 stick butter

3 cloves garlic, minced

1/3 cup Parmesan cheese, grated

1 tsp. ground black pepper

2 tbsp. chopped parsley

2 qt. canola oil

Parmesan Garlic Wings

Directions

1. Place the Copper Chef on medium-high heat. Fill halfway with canola oil. Heat the oil to 365° F.

2. Place the fry basket carefully into the Copper Chef. Add the wings in 3 batches. Cook for about 6 minutes or until golden and crispy.

3. In a clean Copper Chef, melt the butter and add the garlic. Cook for 2 or 3 minutes and then remove from the heat.

4. Add the rest of the ingredients into the pan and stir well. Add the wings and toss until coated.

5. Serve.

Eric's Tip: Go against the grain and serve with marinara sauce instead of ranch or bleu cheese dressing.

SERVES 2

Ingredients

6 slices bread

4 slices roasted turkey

4 slices ham

4 slices Swiss cheese

4 slices American cheese

4 eggs

¼ cup milk

1 tsp. salt

½ tsp. ground black pepper

2 qt. canola oil

Monte Cristo Americano

Directions

1. Place the Copper Chef on medium-high heat and fill halfway with canola oil. Heat the oil to 365° F. Carefully place the fry basket into the Copper Chef.

2. Mix the eggs and milk in a bowl. Assemble the sandwiches: layer 1 slice bread, 1 slice Swiss, 2 slices ham, 1 slice Swiss, 1 slice bread, 2 slices American, 2 slices turkey, and 1 slice bread. Repeat to make the second sandwich.

3. Cut the sandwiches into quarters. Use wooden toothpicks to secure.

4. Dip the sandwich sections into the egg batter, draining off the excess. Then, using tongs, carefully place into the hot oil and cook on both sides.

5. Season with salt and black pepper before serving.

Eric's Tip: A time-honored way to serve Monte Cristos is to dust the sandwiches with powdered sugar and then serve them with a side of strawberry jam.

SERVES 4

Ingredients

1 lb. eye round beef, cut into ½" steaks

½ tsp. salt

½ tsp. ground black pepper, to season steak

1 cup flour

2 eggs

2 tbsp. milk

1 cup breadcrumbs

1 tsp. granulated garlic

1 tsp. granulated onion

1 tsp. sea salt

1 tsp. ground black pepper

2 qt. canola oil

Gravy:

3 tbsp. butter

3 tbsp. flour

2 cups milk

1 cup chicken stock

1 sprig thyme

1 bay leaf

½ tsp. ground black pepper

½ tsp. salt

Country-Fried Steak

Directions

1. Place the steaks on a counter with plastic wrap on top. Pound them with a meat mallet until thin and tender.

2. Season each steak with salt and black pepper. In one dish, place the flour. In a second dish, beat the eggs with the milk and set aside. In a third dish, mix the breadcrumbs with the seasonings.

3. Dust the steaks with the flour, then dip each steak into the eggs, and finally into the breadcrumbs. Set aside.

4. Place the Copper Chef on high heat. Add canola oil until pan is filled halfway. Using tongs, place the breaded steaks into the Copper Chef one at a time and cook until golden. Repeat until all are done.

5. In a clean Copper Chef, melt the butter and add the flour. Stir. Cook for about 2 minutes. Slowly add the milk. Using a whisk, incorporate the milk with the flour and butter. Add the stock and the thyme, bay leaf, salt, and black pepper. Cook for about 20 minutes on low.

6. Place the steaks on a plate and top with gravy.

Eric's Tip: Serve on a fresh, crusty baguette & top with lettuce and tomato for an awesome Country-Fried Steak Po' Boy Sandwich. You can also substitute the steak for chicken or turkey cutlets.

Ingredients

4 chicken thighs

4 chicken legs

2 split chicken breasts, cut in half

1 qt. buttermilk

3 cups flour

3 tbsp. paprika

2 tbsp. sea salt

1 tbsp. ground black pepper

2 tbsp. onion powder

2 tbsp. garlic powder

1 tbsp. cumin

½ tsp. turmeric

1 tsp. cayenne pepper

1 tsp. poultry seasoning

2 qt. canola oil

Fried Chicken

Directions

1. Soak the chicken in the buttermilk. Refrigerate for 4 hours.

2. Mix the rest of the ingredients except for canola oil in a pan. Set aside.

3. Place the Copper Chef on medium-high heat. Fill halfway with canola oil. Heat the oil to 365° F.

4. Carefully place the fry basket into the Copper Chef.

5. Remove the chicken from the buttermilk and dip into the flour mix. Shake off excess and place into the hot oil carefully, in batches (3-4 pieces per batch). Caution: the oil will be HOT!

6. Cook for about 10 minutes or until the chicken is thoroughly cooked and golden.

7. Serve.

Eric's Tip: Adding Louisiana-style hot sauce to the buttermilk marinade gives this a nice southern kick.

Chicken Milanese with Arugula and Fennel Salad

Ingredients

3 tbsp. olive oil

4 (6 oz.) chicken breasts, boneless and skinless

½ cup flour

3 eggs, beaten

1½ cups seasoned breadcrumbs

4 cups baby arugula

1 bulb of fennel, sliced paper thin

1 ripe tomato, diced

3 tbsp. extra virgin olive oil

1 tbsp. red wine vinegar

1 fresh lemon, halved

Parmesan cheese, grated

salt and pepper

Directions

1. Place chicken breasts between two pieces of plastic film and pound to ¼-inch thickness.

2. Season with salt and pepper.

3. Beat eggs in a bowl. In another bowl, place seasoned breadcrumbs. In a third bowl, place flour.

4. Dust chicken with flour, shaking off excess. Dip into beaten egg, then coat with seasoned breadcrumbs.

5. Place the Copper Chef on medium-high heat with olive oil. Sauté chicken in batches for 3-4 minutes on each side until cooked through and golden brown.

6. Hold in a 150° F oven on a baking rack until ready to plate.

7. In a separate bowl, combine fennel, tomato, extra virgin olive oil, and vinegar. Toss well and season with salt and pepper.

8. Just before plating, toss fennel salad and arugula. Use as a bed for the warm chicken.

9. Garnish with Parmesan cheese and lemon.

Eric's Tip: Next time you go on a picnic, try this recipe instead of the usual cold fried chicken. After the chicken is cooked, place the chicken on a baking rack in a sheet tray. This way, it won't get soggy while it cools.

Indulge!

Deep-Fried Desserts

Fried Chocolate Cream-Filled Cookies

Fried Brownies

Glazed Doughnuts

Pumpkin Doughnuts

Apple Fritters

Zeppole

Along with being able to fry the standards like fried chicken and French fries, let's not forget how delicious fried desserts are! Donuts, brownies, even candy bars and cookies are easy to fry in your Copper Chef and accompanying fry basket because of its perfect depth for deep-frying. Just when you thought dessert couldn't be more decadent...

Fried Chocolate Cream-Filled Cookies

Ingredients

18 cream-filled chocolate cookies

2 eggs

½ cup milk

1 cup flour

¼ tsp. nutmeg

1 tbsp. sugar

½ tsp. cinnamon

1 tsp. baking powder

2 qt. canola oil

Directions

1. Place the Copper Chef on medium-high heat. Fill halfway with canola oil. Heat the oil to 365° F.

2. Place the fry basket carefully into the Copper Chef.

3. In a bowl, mix the eggs and milk together. Slowly mix in the rest of the ingredients, except canola oil, until all incorporated.

4. Dip the cookies into the batter and shake off excess batter. Using tongs, carefully drop the cookies into the oil. Cook until lightly golden.

5. Repeat until finished. Serve.

Eric's Tip: A tall glass of cold milk is still the best companion to this delicious treat. You are never too old to dunk!

Ingredients

1 box brownie mix

3 eggs

¾ cup milk

1 ½ cup flour

1 tsp. vanilla

1 tbsp. sugar

2 tsp. baking powder

2 qt. canola oil

Fried Brownies

Directions

1. Following the directions on the box, make the brownies and set aside to cool.

2. In a bowl, mix the eggs and milk. Slowly mix in the rest of the ingredients, except canola oil, and set aside.

3. Place the Copper Chef on medium-high heat, then fill halfway with canola oil. Heat the oil to 365° F.

4. Place the fry basket carefully into the Copper Chef.

5. Cut the brownies into 2" by 2" squares. Dip them into the batter and shake off excess. Carefully drop into the hot oil using tongs. Cook until lightly golden.

6. Repeat until all the brownies are cooked. Serve.

Eric's Tip: Sometimes after a tough day, I make an ice cream sandwich out of these!

Glazed Doughnuts

Ingredients

Doughnuts:

1 cup milk

½ tbsp. dry active yeast

2 eggs

¾ stick butter, melted

2 tbsp. sugar

½ tsp. salt

3 cups flour, all-purpose

2 quarts canola oil

Glaze:

2 cups confectioners sugar

1 tsp. vanilla extract

4 tbsp. hot water

Directions

1. In an electric mixer using the dough blade, add all of the doughnut ingredients, except canola oil. Mix on low to start, then move to medium speed. When the dough forms a ball, remove from the mixer and put into a clean bowl. Cover the bowl with a towel and put in a warm place until it doubles in size (about 1 hour).

2. After the dough has doubled in size (proofed), place on a floured surface and roll to about an inch thick. With a doughnut cutter, cut out the doughnuts. Place the doughnuts on a floured pan for about 45-minutes until doubled in size.

3. Place the Copper Chef on medium-high heat. Add the fry basket and fill halfway with canola oil.

4. Carefully place the doughnuts into the fry basket using tongs. Cook on both sides until golden brown.

5. Place the doughnuts on a baking rack to cool.

6. Make the glaze by mixing all the glaze ingredients in a bowl.

7. When the doughnuts are cool, pour the glaze over them.

8. Serve.

Eric's Tip: Proofing (when dough doubles in size) in your oven works great. Simply preheat the oven to 200° F. As soon as it reaches temperature, turn it off. This creates the perfect warm and dry zone for proofing.

SERVES 6-8

Ingredients

3 cups all-purpose flour

2 tsp. baking powder

½ tsp. salt

1 tsp. cinnamon

¼ tsp. nutmeg

1 egg

¾ cup sugar

⅔ cup milk

2 tbsp. melted butter

½ tbsp. vanilla extract

⅔ cup pumpkin purée

2 qt. canola oil

Cinnamon & Sugar Coating:

1 cup sugar

2 tbsp. cinnamon

Pumpkin Doughnuts

Directions

1. In a bowl, mix together the dry ingredients. In another bowl, mix together the wet ingredients, except for canola oit. Set aside.

2. Make a hole in the dry ingredients; pour the wet ingredients into the middle. Mix until incorporated.

3. Place in the refrigerator for 2 hours.

4. Place the Copper Chef on high heat and fill with canola oil halfway. Place fry basket into the Copper Chef. Heat the canola oil to 365° F.

5. Roll the doughnut dough out and use a round cutter to make the doughnuts.

6. Carefully fry the doughnuts until golden on all sides.

7. In a separate bowl, mix the sugar and cinnamon together. Dip the hot doughnuts in the cinnamon & sugar coating.

8. Serve.

Eric's Tip: My preference is to dunk these doughnuts in hot mulled cider instead of coffee!

Ingredients

2 cups all-purpose flour

½ cup granulated sugar

2 tsp. baking powder

1½ tsp. ground cinnamon

¼ tsp. nutmeg

½ tsp. sea salt

2 large eggs

¾ cup milk

2 tbsp. honey

2 tbsp. melted butter

1 tsp. vanilla extract

3 apples, cored and diced small

1 cup confectioners sugar, for dusting

2 qt. canola oil

Apple Fritters

Directions

1. In a bowl, mix the dry ingredients and set aside. In another bowl, mix the wet ingredients (except canola oil), and then add slowly to the dry ingredients. Fold in the diced apples.

2. Place the Copper Chef on high heat and fill with canola oil halfway. Heat the canola oil to 365° F.

3. Place the fry basket into the Copper Chef.

4. With a spoon, carefully drop spoonfuls of batter into the hot oil. Cook until lightly golden.

5. Dust with confectioners sugar before serving.

Eric's Tip: My kids love when I serve these with caramel sauce and little side dishes of chocolate chips, mini marshmallows, and chopped nuts to dip!

Ingredients

1½ cups water

1 tbsp. yeast

1 tbsp. honey

1 tsp. vanilla

3 cups flour

1 tbsp. olive oil

2 tsp. sea salt

1 cup confectioners sugar, for dusting

2 qt. canola oil

Zeppole

Directions

1. In an electric mixer, add the ingredients in order. Turn the mixer to low and mix until the dough forms a ball.

2. On a floured surface, place the dough down and flour the dough. Roll the dough out and cut into small pieces.

3. Place the Copper Chef on high heat and fill with canola oil halfway. Heat the canola oil to 365° F.

4. Place the fry basket carefully into the Copper Chef.

5. Carefully drop the dough in spoonfuls into the hot oil. Cook until lightly golden.

6. Dust with confectioners sugar before serving.

Eric's Tip: Zeppoles are also great filled. Add some vanilla pudding to a zip-top bag, cut off the corner and use it as a piping bag to fill each zeppole after it's cooled.

Mouthwatering
Oven-Roasted Recipes

Mom's Meatloaf

Roast Prime Rib of Beef

Spicy Cowboy Steak

Roast Beef

Classic Roasted Chicken

Spicy Brick Chicken

Orange Brine Turkey Breast

Miso-Glazed Salmon

BBQ Baby Back Ribs

Jerk Ribs

Roasted Pork Loin

Bacon-Wrapped Roast Pork

Rosemary Rack of Lamb

The Copper Chef is great for oven-roasting. What I especially like about roasting is that it is great for large gatherings because most of the work is done in the oven and, most of the time, just needs to be timed, but not monitored. Thanks to the square shape and its depth, you can oven-roast most anything in Copper Chef. We give you an accessory that we call a steamer tray. That same tray happens to also work great as a roasting rack for your whole chickens and roasts! It's great for meatloaf, too, because it keeps the loaf out of the grease for better overall results.

Ingredients

2 lb. ground pork / veal / beef mix

¼ cup celery, minced

¼ cup carrot, minced

¼ cup onion, minced

1 clove garlic, chopped

1 tsp. dry thyme

1 ½ cups breadcrumbs

1 cup ketchup

1 tbsp. steak sauce

2 tbsp. Worcestershire sauce

2 large eggs

salt and pepper

Mom's Meatloaf

Directions

1. Preheat the oven to 350° F.

2. Combine onion, carrot, celery, garlic, thyme, breadcrumbs, Worcestershire sauce, steak sauce, eggs, and half of the ketchup.

3. Add ground meat, salt, and pepper. Mix well.

4. Form ground beef mixture into a loaf. Place onto the steamer tray in the Copper Chef.

5. Spread remaining ketchup on top of loaf.

6. Bake in the oven for 40-50 minutes, or until internal temperature reaches 150° F.

Eric's Tip: I prefer to use fresh breadcrumbs. Simply put bread or rolls into a blender or a food processor and blend them to a fine consistency.

Ingredients

4 garlic cloves, peeled

2 tbsp. Dijon mustard

1 tbsp. paprika

5 lb. beef, prime rib

1 tbsp. sea salt

½ tbsp. ground black pepper

3 tbsp. olive oil

½ cup red wine

1 cup beef stock

6-7 shakes of Worcestershire sauce

2 tbsp. butter

Roast Prime Rib of Beef

Directions

1. Preheat the oven to 400° F.

2. In a food processor, make a paste out of garlic, Dijon, and paprika. Set aside.

3. Season the roast with salt and pepper.

4. Preheat the Copper Chef on high heat. Add olive oil when hot.

5. Sear the roast until browned on all sides.

6. Apply the paste to the top of the roast with a basting brush or silicone paddle.

7. Cook in the oven until it reaches about 130-140° F (suggested).

8. Remove the roast from the pan and set aside.

9. Place the Copper Chef back on the stovetop on medium-high heat. Deglaze the pan with red wine. When the wine has reduced, add the beef stock. Cook for about 5 minutes, then turn off the heat source.

10. Add 6 or 7 shakes of Worcestershire sauce and stir in the butter.

11. Once the roast has rested for about 15 minutes, it is ready to serve with the reduction sauce.

Eric's Tip: For a delicious twist, substitute the butter for Boursin or Roquefort cheese.

Spicy Cowboy Steak

Ingredients

1½ lb. beef rib steak, bone-in

1 tsp. sea salt

½ tsp. ground black pepper

2 tbsp. olive oil

1 tsp. ground coffee

½ tsp. cayenne pepper, ground

1 tbsp. brown sugar

3 garlic cloves, minced

1 tbsp. butter

1 sprig rosemary

Directions

1. Preheat the oven to 450° F.

2. Season the steak with sea salt and black pepper.

3. Place the Copper Chef on high heat. Once heated, add the olive oil. Sear the steak for about 2 minutes on each side.

4. In a small bowl, mix the ground coffee, cayenne, and brown sugar well. Using a basting brush, rub steak with mixture.

5. Place the garlic, butter, and rosemary on the steak. Place the Copper Chef into the oven.

6. Cook for about 15-20 minutes or until it reaches 130° F (for medium-rare).

7. Let the steak rest for 10 minutes before serving.

Eric's Tip: Using a double-cut pork chop is a good, cost-effective alternative. Just cook to 165° F.

Ingredients

3 lb. beef roast, eye of round

2 tsp. sea salt

2 tbsp. olive oil

2 sprigs thyme, chopped

2 sprigs rosemary, chopped

2 garlic cloves, peeled and minced

2 tbsp. cracked black pepper

½ cup Parmesan cheese

½ cup butter, softened

1 tsp. onion powder

½ tsp. garlic powder

2 tbsp. fresh horseradish

Roast Beef

Directions

1. Preheat the oven to 400° F.

2. Season the roast with sea salt.

3. Preheat the Copper Chef and then add olive oil. Sear the roast until browned on all sides.

4. Chop the herbs. Mix in a bowl with the remaining ingredients.

5. Apply mixture to the roast with a silicone paddle or basting brush.

6. Place in the oven and cook until about 135° F.

7. Let the roast rest for 15 minutes. Slice thin before serving.

Eric's Tip: This recipe works great with a center-cut, boneless pork loin roast. Just increase internal temperature to 165° F.

Ingredients

3-4 lb. roasting chicken

3 tbsp. fresh thyme, chopped

3 tbsp. softened butter

1 tbsp. black peppercorns, fresh cracked

1 tsp. dry sage

1 tsp. turmeric

1 fresh lemon, zest and juiced

salt and pepper

Classic Roasted Chicken

Directions

1. Preheat the oven to 425° F.

2. In a bowl, combine thyme, butter, peppercorns, sage, turmeric, lemon zest, and lemon juice.

3. Season inside of cavity with salt and pepper, then place juiced lemon halves inside.

4. Gently massage citrus herb mixture into skin of chicken.

5. Using kitchen string, tie the legs so the chicken is nice and compact.

6. Place the chicken in the Copper Chef.

7. Roast chicken in the oven for 20 minutes. Reduce the temperature to 350° and continue roasting for another 30-50 minutes, or until an internal temperature of 160° F.

8. Let chicken rest for at least 10 minutes before carving.

Eric's Tip: Don't be afraid to place your hand under the skin and carefully separate it from the meat. You can take some of the citrus herb mixture and season under there for extra flavor.

Ingredients

1 (3-4 lb.) roasting chicken

1 tbsp. paprika

1 tsp. cumin

1 clove garlic, crushed

1 tsp. fresh thyme, chopped

1 tsp. turmeric

1 tsp. cayenne pepper

¼ cup olive oil

2 tsp. salt

1 tsp. ground black pepper

1 fresh lime, zest and juice

Spicy Brick Chicken

Directions

1. Preheat the oven to 375° F.

2. Using heavy kitchen shears or a chef's knife, cut down either side of the chicken back bone. Remove.

3. Flatten the chicken and remove the breast bone and ribcage. Place the chicken in a large zip-top bag or container.

4. Combine all remaining ingredients. Mix well. Add to chicken and marinate for 1-6 hours.

5. Heat Copper Chef. Place chicken in the pan, skin side down. Sear for 5-8 minutes.

6. Place a foil-wrapped brick on top of the chicken. Put the Copper Chef pan into the preheated oven.

7. Roast for 25-35 minutes, or until an internal temperature of 160° F.

8. Let the chicken rest for 10 minutes. Remove brick before serving.

Eric's Tip: Removing the back bone and flattening the chicken is called "Spatchcocking." This exposes more skin to get it crispier; plus, it reduces the cooking time.

Ingredients

Brine (optional):

1½ qt. cold water

½ cup kosher salt

½ cup sugar

2 cloves garlic, smashed

2 bay leaves

1 tbsp. whole peppercorns

2 fresh oranges, zested and juice squeezed

4-6 lb. turkey breast, bone-in

1. Combine all ingredients and mix well.

2. Place turkey into a large zip-top bag or container. Pour mixture over turkey.

3. Make sure the turkey is completely submerged in brine. Let soak 6-12 hours.

Herb Rub:

1 tbsp. fresh rosemary, chopped

1 tbsp. fresh sage, chopped

2 tbsp. fresh thyme, chopped

1 tbsp. black pepper

1 tsp. paprika

2 cloves garlic, chopped

6 tbsp. butter, softened

Pan Gravy:

1 yellow onion, chopped

1 carrot, chopped

2 stalks celery, chopped

3 cloves garlic

1 bay leaf

1 cup water

1 cup chicken stock

¼ cup white wine

1 tbsp. butter

1 tbsp. flour

Orange Brine Turkey Breast

Directions

1. Preheat the oven to 400° F.

2. Combine all herb rub ingredients in a bowl. Mix well.

3. Remove turkey from brine. Pat dry. Add vegetables, garlic, bay leaf, and water to the Copper Chef. Place the turkey breast on top.

4. Gently loosen skin with your hand and spread half of the herb rub mixture under skin. Then spread remaining mixture over top of skin.

5. Place the turkey breast in the Copper Chef. Place into the preheated oven. After 20 minutes, reduce temperature to 325° F and cook for another 60-70 minutes or until internal temperature reaches 155° F (if skin gets too brown, cover with foil).

6. Remove the turkey from the Copper Chef and set aside.

7. Pour off pan juices and skim fat.

8. Place Copper Chef pan back on the stovetop burner. Deglaze pan with wine. Add butter and melt. Whisk in flour until smooth.

9. Add stock and pan drippings. Simmer for 8-10 minutes.

10. Slice the turkey and serve with gravy.

Eric's Tip: Brining your turkey before roasting it gives you a more tender and juicier result. If you don't have time to brine the turkey, it's still going to taste delicious. I've seen some supermarkets now sell turkey breasts that are already brined. It costs a little more, but it is worth it.

Ingredients

4 (6 oz.) salmon fillets or steaks

1 tbsp. olive oil

1/3 cup yellow miso

¼ cup orange juice

1 ½ tbsp. sherry wine

2 tbsp. soy sauce

1 tbsp. honey

1 tbsp. ground ginger

1 tbsp. fresh cilantro, chopped

Miso-Glazed Salmon

Directions

1. Combine olive oil, yellow miso, orange juice, sherry wine, soy sauce, honey, ginger, and cilantro. Mix well.

2. Marinate salmon in miso marinade for at least 30 minutes.

3. Place salmon in the Copper Chef. Broil on high for 3-5 minutes per side or until desired doneness.

BBQ Baby Back Ribs

SERVES 4

Ingredients

2 racks baby back pork ribs, cut in half

water, to boil ribs

2 tbsp. granulated garlic

2 tbsp. granulated onion

1 tbsp. ground cumin

1 tbsp. ground coriander

1 tbsp. sea salt

1 tbsp. paprika

1 tbsp. ground black pepper

1½ cups BBQ sauce

Directions

1. Place the ribs into the Copper Chef and cover them with water. Place the Copper Chef on high heat. Cover. Bring the ribs to a boil and then lower the heat. Simmer for 1 hour.

2. Preheat the oven to 350° F.

3. In a bowl, mix the spices together to make a rub.

4. Remove the ribs and place them on a cookie sheet. Rub the spices onto the ribs and put into the oven for 15 minutes.

5. Remove the ribs and brush generously with BBQ sauce. Return to the oven for an additional 15 minutes before serving.

Eric's Tip: My friend told me she always boils her ribs before roasting. I'm always up for trying methods that I have not used. Well, she was right, so now I use her method. My favorite type of BBQ sauce is a Carolina mustard and vinegar style.

Ingredients

2 racks baby back ribs, cut in half

4 tbsp. olive oil

Jerk Seasoning:

½ cup brown sugar

3 tbsp. onion powder

2 tbsp. allspice

2 tbsp. cinnamon

3 tbsp. paprika

2 tbsp. dry thyme

2 tsp. cayenne pepper

3 tbsp. sea salt

2 tbsp. ground black pepper

Jerk Ribs

Directions

1. Preheat the oven to 325° F.

2. In a bowl, mix the brown sugar and spices together to make a jerk seasoning.

3. Place the ribs into the Copper Chef. Rub with olive oil and then with the jerk seasoning.

4. Place the Copper Chef into the oven.

5. Cook the ribs for about 2½ hours or until tender.

6. Remove the ribs and serve.

Eric's Tip: Everyone has a different tolerance to spice. I used cayenne but there are so many hot peppers in the world! Feel free to try mincing one or two hot peppers instead of adding the cayenne.

Ingredients

1 (3-4 lb.) center cut pork loin

2 cups water

¼ cup salt

¼ cup sugar

½ tbsp. whole black peppercorns

1 bay leaf

1 tbsp. olive oil

1 tsp. dry rosemary

1 tsp. dry thyme

1 tbsp. salt, for rub

2 tbsp. fennel seeds, crushed

½ tbsp. ground black pepper

Roasted Pork Loin

Directions

1. Preheat the oven to 425° F.

2. Combine water, salt, sugar, peppercorns, and bay leaf in a large zip-top bag. Swish around to combine. Place pork loin in bag and brine for 1-3 hours.

3. Remove pork from brine and pat dry. Using a sharp knife, make shallow slashes every 1/8 inch or so across the top of the pork. This will allow the fat to render and a nice crust to form.

4. Rub the olive oil, rosemary, thyme, salt, black pepper, and fennel seeds into the pork.

5. Place pork in the Copper Chef pan and into the oven for 35-45 minutes, or until internal temperature of 150° F.

6. Let rest for 10 minutes before serving.

Eric's Tip: You can skip the brining step, but if you have the time, it does produce a juicier result.

Bacon-Wrapped Roast Pork

Ingredients

1 lb. bacon

2 lb. pork loin, trimmed

1 tsp. sea salt

1 tsp. ground black pepper

2 tbsp. olive oil

Sauce:

1 shallot, peeled and diced

2 Granny Smith apples, diced

¼ cup apple cider

¾ cup chicken stock

2 sprigs tarragon

1 bay leaf

2 tbsp. butter

Directions

1. Preheat the oven to 375° F.

2. Season the pork loin with sea salt and black pepper.

3. Lay the bacon out 2 slices per row. Place the pork loin in the middle and start wrapping the bacon around the top.

4. Place the Copper Chef on medium-high heat. When the pan is hot, add the olive oil and sear all sides of the roast. Place the roast into the oven.

5. When the roast has an internal temperature of 160° F, remove from the oven and set on a plate.

6. Place the Copper Chef back on medium-high heat. Add the shallots and apples; sweat for 3 or 4 minutes.

7. Pour in the apple cider, chicken stock, tarragon, and bay leaf. Cook for about 5 minutes. Add the butter and cook for 2 more minutes.

8. Slice the roast and serve with the sauce.

Eric's Tip: I prefer uncured, thick-cut bacon, but when it comes to bacon… there is no wrong decision!

Rosemary Rack of Lamb

SERVES 2-4

Ingredients

2 tbsp. olive oil

2 tsp. sea salt, California

1 tsp. ground black pepper

2 (1-1¼ lb.) racks of lamb

4 garlic cloves, minced

4 sprigs rosemary, chopped

1 tbsp. Dijon mustard

2 tsp. cumin, ground

2 tsp. coriander, ground

2 sprigs additional rosemary, chopped, for garnish

Directions

1. Preheat the oven to 450° F.

2. Add the olive oil to the preheated Copper Chef.

3. Season the lamb with sea salt and black pepper. Sear on all sides.

4. Rub the seared lamb racks with Dijon mustard, cumin, coriander, garlic, and rosemary.

5. Place the lamb into the oven. Cook for about 20-25 minutes (for rare to medium-rare) or until desired internal temperature.

6. Let the rack rest for 10 minutes before cutting.

7. Before serving, sprinkle remaining fresh rosemary over lamb.

Eric's Tip: Wrap the top half of the rack with aluminum foil to keep it from getting too dark.

Simply
Sautéed

Philly Cheesesteak

Shrimp and Saffron Risotto

Chicken Alfredo

Texas Smokehouse Stuffed Burger

Chicken Paprikash

**Chicken Breasts
with Tomato Tapenade**

**Cuban Pork Asado
with Black Bean Relish**

**Pan-Seared Herb Pork Chops
with Apple Slaw**

Spicy Mussels

Summer Clams

**Pork Marsala
with Mushrooms and Spinach**

Crab Cakes

Pan-Seared Scallops Over Greens

Hot and Sweet Sausage and Peppers

Tilapia Francese

**Pan-Seared Tuna
with Mango Pineapple Salsa**

Salmon Burgers

Flounder in Saffron Tomato Broth

**Prosciutto-Wrapped Cod
with Edamame Salad**

Fusilli and Clams

Linguini Carbonara

Penne alla Vodka

The word sauté comes from the French verb "sauter," which means "to jump." When you sauté, you use a hot pan and a minimal amount of fat or oil to make your food "jump" a bit as you cook it and shake it around in the pan. Sautéing in the Copper Chef is great because its square shape and high sides help you move the food around the pan quickly, without any of it falling over the sides. Although not a traditional size or shape for sautéing, I think you'll agree that the Copper Chef actually works best.

Ingredients

3 tbsp. olive oil

1 lb. sliced beef

1 onion, peeled and sliced

½ red pepper, seeded and sliced

½ green bell pepper, seeded and sliced

2 cloves garlic, peeled and sliced

1 tbsp. soy sauce

2 sub rolls

6 slices provolone

Philly Cheesesteak

Directions

1. Place the Copper Chef on high heat. When the pan is hot, add the olive oil and sear the beef.

2. Remove the beef and set aside. Place the onions and red and green peppers into the Copper Chef. Sauté until tender. Add the garlic and cook for 3 more minutes.

3. Add the beef back into the pan with the soy sauce. Stir. Remove from heat.

4. Slice the sub rolls. Divide the beef into each sub roll. Top each with 3 slices of provolone cheese. Put under the broiler to melt before serving.

Eric's Tip: In Philly they love the "cheese wiz" from a can drizzled on the meat. Feel free to skip the provolone and try the Philly way.

Shrimp and Saffron Risotto

SERVES 6

Ingredients

2 tbsp. butter

2 tbsp. olive oil

1 small onion, minced

1 shallot, peeled and minced

pinch of saffron threads

1 cup Arborio rice

1 bay leaf

2 sprigs tarragon

1 tsp. sea salt

½ tsp. ground black pepper

5 cups shrimp broth or chicken stock

½ cup white wine

2 lb. shrimp, peeled and deveined

¼ cup Parmigiano-Reggiano, grated

juice of half a lemon

2 tsp. lemon zest

Directions

1. Place the Copper Chef on medium heat. Add olive oil and butter. Add the onions and shallots. Sauté for about 3 minutes.

2. Add the saffron and cook for another minute. Add the rice and coat well with the olive oil, stirring consistently.

3. Add the white wine, tarragon, and bay leaf. Continue stirring constantly until wine is absorbed. Add the broth or stock ¼ cup at a time until absorbed.

4. Season shrimp with salt and pepper. Stir into the risotto. Cover for 2-3 minutes on low heat until shrimp are cooked and liquid has been absorbed.

5. Remove from the heat. Stir in the Parmigiano-Reggiano cheese and lemon juice. Sprinkle with lemon zest before serving.

Eric's Tip: Making risotto is a labor of love. The constant stirring is the key to a creamy risotto. As you stir, the starches break off from the Arborio rice and thicken the sauce. Trust me, your efforts will be rewarded!

Chicken Alfredo

SERVES 4

Ingredients

2 chicken breasts, trimmed and cubed small

3 tbsp. olive oil

4 cloves garlic, peeled and minced

½ cup chicken stock

½ lb. fettuccine, cooked al dente (firm)

3 cups heavy cream

3 tbsp. butter

1 tsp. sea salt

½ tsp. ground black pepper

2 cups grated Parmigiano-Reggiano

1 tbsp. lemon zest

Directions

1. Place the Copper Chef on medium heat. Add the olive oil and sauté the chicken for about 4 minutes.

2. Add the garlic; cook for about 3 minutes before adding the chicken stock. When the chicken stock is reduced by half, add the heavy cream and bring to a boil. Reduce heat to a simmer and add the butter. Simmer until the sauce is reduced by about half. Turn off the heat.

3. Add the pasta to the pan. Coat well with the cream sauce.

4. Toss in Parmigiano-Reggiano cheese, lemon zest, sea salt, and black pepper.

5. Serve immediately.

Eric's Tip: Sometimes I enjoy this served over a fresh baked potato instead of pasta. Feel free to substitute shrimp for chicken.

Ingredients

Onion Rings:

1 onion, peeled and sliced

1 cup milk

2 cups flour

½ tbsp. sea salt

½ tbsp. ground black pepper

Burger:

1½ lb. ground beef

1 tsp. sea salt

½ tsp. ground black pepper

½ tsp. granulated garlic

½ tsp. granulated onion

4 tbsp. BBQ sauce

4 strips bacon, cooked and cut in half

4 oz. cheddar cheese, in 4 chunks

3 tbsp. olive oil

4 brioche rolls

3 tbsp. butter

2 qt. canola oil

Texas Smokehouse Stuffed Burger

Directions

1. Soak the onion rings in the milk. In a separate bowl, season the flour with sea salt & black pepper.

2. Place the Copper Chef on high heat. Fill halfway with canola oil. When the temperature reaches 365° F, dip the onions into the seasoned flour. Shake off any excess and carefully drop into the hot oil. Cook until golden. Set aside.

3. In a bowl, mix the ground beef, sea salt, black pepper, garlic, and onion. Form 4 balls. Poke a hole in the center of each and insert a chunk of cheddar cheese. Cover the cheese with the ground beef mixture. Press down to form burgers.

4. Place Copper Chef on medium-high heat. Brush the brioche rolls with the butter and toast. Set aside.

5. Add the olive oil to the Copper Chef. Cook the burgers for 3-4 minutes on each side or until desired doneness.

6. Place the burgers on the brioche rolls. Top each burger with BBQ sauce, 2 half strips of bacon, and a couple of onion rings before serving.

Eric's Tip: Frozen onion rings (baked or deep-fried) work just as well if you want to save some time.

Ingredients

3 tbsp. olive oil

2½ lb. chicken breast, cubed

2 cups thinly sliced onions

1 large shallot, minced

¾ cup canned tomatoes, diced

2 tbsp. Hungarian sweet paprika

½ tsp. Hungarian hot paprika or cayenne pepper

1 tsp. dried marjoram

½ tsp. dry thyme

salt and pepper

½ cup sour cream

⅓ cup fresh Italian parsley, chopped

Chicken Paprikash

Directions

1. Place the Copper Chef on medium-high heat. Add the olive oil and brown chicken in small batches for 5-7 minutes each. Set aside.

2. Add onions and shallot. Sauté for 5 minutes until translucent.

3. Add sweet paprika, marjoram, thyme, and hot paprika.

4. Return chicken to the pan. Add diced tomatoes. Reduce heat and simmer for 15-20 minutes. Season with salt and pepper.

5. Remove from heat. Stir in sour cream and parsley before serving.

Eric's Tip: The key to this dish is the sour cream, but if you would like a lighter version, Greek yogurt can be substituted.

Chicken Breasts with Tomato Tapenade

Ingredients

3 tbsp. olive oil

4 bone-in, skin-on split chicken breasts

1 tsp. ground turmeric

pinch of ground cumin

¼ cup roasted pine nuts

½ cup plump sundried tomatoes

½ cup pitted kalamata olives

½ cup small onion, large chopped

½ cup marinated or grilled mushrooms

1 tsp. fresh garlic

salt and pepper, to taste

Directions

1. Preheat the oven to 350° F.

2. In a heated Copper Chef, add enough olive oil to coat the pan.

3. Rub each chicken breast with salt, pepper, turmeric, and cumin.

4. Sear chicken breasts skin side down until they are deep, golden brown.

5. Place pan in the preheated oven. Cook for about 35 min., or until the internal temperature of the chicken is 185° F.

6. Make the tapenade: in a food processor combine pine nuts, sundried tomatoes, olives, onion, mushrooms, garlic, salt, and pepper. Pulse a few times for a chunky consistency.

7. Put a generous portion of the tapenade on top of each breast. Let the chicken sit for about 5 minutes before serving.

Eric's Tip: I like to drizzle each plate with high quality olive oil. This dish is great with couscous and wilted spinach as sides. Optional: Try crumbling some goat cheese around the plate for added flavor.

Cuban Pork Asado with Black Bean Relish

Ingredients

4 (8 oz.) bone-in pork chops

1 cup orange juice

1 cup lime juice

1 tbsp. cumin

4 cloves garlic, smashed

1 tsp. chili flakes

1 tsp. salt

1 tsp. pepper

1 tbsp. honey

3 tbsp. olive oil, for searing

For the relish:

2 cans black beans, rinsed and drained

¼ cup red onion, chopped

¼ cup celery, chopped

1 clove garlic, chopped

1 cup ripe tomato, chopped

1 scallion, chopped

1 tbsp. olive oil

1 tsp. cumin

½ tsp. dry oregano

1 fresh lime, juice and zest

½ tsp. salt

Directions

1. Place pork chops, orange juice, lime juice, cumin, garlic, chili flakes, salt, pepper, and honey in a zip-top bag. Marinate for 30 minutes.

2. For the black bean relish: combine black beans, red onion, celery, garlic, tomato, scallion, olive oil, cumin, lime juice, oregano, and salt. Refrigerate for 15 minutes.

3. Remove pork chops from marinade and pat dry with a paper towel. Place the Copper Chef on medium-high heat. Add olive oil and sauté for 5-8 minutes per side until done.

4. Serve with the black bean relish.

Eric's Tip: Asado is Latin for "barbeque." Adding the citrus juice gives it a Cuban twist. Just add a side of yellow rice, and you're all set!

Pan-Seared Herb Pork Chops with Apple Slaw

SERVES 4

Ingredients

4 (8 oz.) bone-in pork chops

3 tsp. dry sage

1 tsp. dry basil

1 tsp. dry oregano

½ tsp. ground pepper

1 tsp. salt

4 tbsp. olive oil

2 Granny Smith apples, julienned

4 cups shredded green cabbage

1 cup carrots, julienned

2 tbsp. cider vinegar

½ cup Greek yogurt

½ tsp. salt

1 tsp. ground pepper

2 tbsp. honey

Directions

1. In a small bowl, combine sage, basil, oregano, salt, ground pepper, and olive oil.

2. Coat pork chops with herb mixture. Marinate for 30 minutes.

3. In a separate bowl, combine Granny Smith apples, grain cabbage, carrots, cider vinegar, Greek yogurt, salt, pepper, and honey. Mix well and refrigerate for 30 minutes.

4. Place the Copper Chef on medium-high heat. Sear the pork chops for 5-8 minutes on each side.

5. Serve with apple slaw.

Eric's Tip: Toss the apples immediately in the vinegar to prevent oxidation. I also like to switch it up a bit and use Bosc pears when they are in season.

Ingredients

2-3 lb. mussels, cleaned and beard removed

3 tbsp. olive oil

2 cloves garlic, smashed

2 tsp. chili flakes

¾ cup white wine

2 cups canned Italian tomatoes, diced

4 tbsp. fresh Italian parsley chopped

salt and pepper

Spicy Mussels

Directions

1. Place the Copper Chef on medium heat. Add olive oil, garlic, and chili flakes. Cook until garlic turns light brown.

2. Deglaze with white wine. Add tomatoes, salt, and pepper.

3. Bring sauce to a simmer, then add mussels and parsley.

4. Cover. Raise the heat to medium-high and cook for 5-7 minutes or until mussels open.

Eric's Tip: Depending on what is fresh in the market, you can substitute clams, shrimp, or scallops. If you are feeling extra adventurous, mix them up. They all have similar cooking times. Don't forget the crusty bread!

Ingredients

3 tbsp. butter

3 cloves garlic, minced

4 dozen clams, in-shell, cleaned

1 bunch scallions, chopped

1 cup white wine

½ cup clam broth

1 bay leaf

2 tbsp. cilantro, chopped

½ tsp. sea salt

½ tsp. ground black pepper

¼ tsp. red pepper flakes

juice of 2 lemons

Summer Clams

Directions

1. Place the Copper Chef on medium heat and melt the butter. Add the garlic and sweat for 2-3 minutes.

2. Add the rest of the ingredients. Stir and cover.

3. Cook until the clams have opened. Remove the clams to a serving bowl, leaving the liquid in the Copper Chef.

4. Reduce the liquid by about a third. Pour over the clams before serving.

Eric's Tip: The key to this recipe is to use the absolute freshest seafood possible. If you can't find clams, then use mussels. If you can't find mussels, then use shrimp. Serving over pasta or risotto turns this into an amazing meal!

Pork Marsala with Mushrooms and Spinach

SERVES 2

Ingredients

4 (3 oz.) pork cutlets, pounded thin

½ cup flour

1 pinch salt

1 pinch pepper

1 tsp. dried oregano

2 tbsp. olive oil

2 tbsp. butter

½ lb. cremini mushrooms, sliced thick

8 oz. baby spinach

½ cup heavy cream

½ cup beef stock

⅓ cup sweet Marsala wine

¼ tsp. chili flakes

1 clove garlic, smashed

salt and pepper

Directions

1. In a large bowl, combine flour, pinch of salt and pepper, and oregano. Lightly dredge the pounded cutlets in this mixture.

2. Place the Copper Chef on medium-high heat. Add the olive oil and butter. When the oil is hot, sear pork cutlets for 2 minutes on each side. Remove and set aside.

3. Sauté mushrooms for 7-9 minutes or until mushrooms have caramelized.

4. Add garlic and sauté for 1 minute.

5. Deglaze the pan with Marsala wine.

6. Add spinach and toss until wilted.

7. Add heavy cream, beef stock, chili flakes, and pork cutlets.

8. Simmer for 8-10 minutes.

9. Adjust seasoning with salt and pepper before serving.

Eric's Tip: Adding in some dried porcini mushrooms reconstituted in the Marsala will add an extra layer of flavor. This dish is fantastic over any kind of pasta, and especially delicious over risotto.

Ingredients

4 egg whites, whipped to soft peaks

1 lb. lump crab meat, drained well

1 tsp. seafood seasoning

1 shallot, minced

½ red pepper, seeded and diced small

⅓ cup mayonnaise

⅓ cup cracker crumbs

1 tbsp. Dijon mustard

2 tbsp. heavy cream

½ tsp. sea salt

½ tsp. ground black pepper

½ cup canola oil

1 cup flour

Crab Cakes

Directions

1. In a medium bowl, whip the egg whites until you achieve soft peaks.

2. Place the crab into a large bowl with all of the ingredients except the flour and canola oil. Mix well.

3. Place the Copper Chef on high heat with ½ cup canola oil.

4. Form the crab cakes and dust with flour.

5. Carefully cook the crab cakes in the Copper Chef until golden on each side.

6. Serve.

Eric's Tip: There is nothing better than serving these crab cakes on a potato roll with a slice of ripe tomato, a dollop of tartar sauce, and a sprinkle of seafood seasoning for a taste of Maryland.

Pan-Seared Scallops Over Greens

SERVES 4

Ingredients

1½ lb. sea scallops, cleaned

1 tsp. sea salt

1 tsp. ground black pepper

3 tbsp. canola oil

6 cups mixed baby greens

1 bulb fennel, shaved

½ red onion, peeled and thinly sliced

Dressing for Greens:

1 shallot, minced

½ tsp. Dijon mustard

3 tbsp. apple cider vinegar

1 sprig fresh tarragon, minced

½ cup extra virgin olive oil

¼ tsp. sea salt

¼ tsp. ground black pepper, to taste

Directions

1. Place the Copper Chef on high heat. Add the canola oil. Pat scallops dry; season with sea salt and black pepper. Sear on each side until golden brown (about 2 or 3 minutes for each side).

2. In a bowl, mix dressing ingredients together. In a separate bowl, toss the greens with the fennel and red onion. Drizzle greens with some of the dressing.

3. Plate the scallops with the salad before serving.

Eric's Tip: I have also done this as a chilled summer salad. Once the scallops are cooked according to the directions, I'll place them in the refrigerator to chill for an hour. You still get that clean, fresh scallop taste without wilting the greens.

Hot and Sweet Sausage and Peppers

SERVES 4-6

Ingredients

4 tbsp. olive oil

1½ lb. sweet sausage, cut into 2-inch pieces

1½ lb. hot sausage, cut into 2-inch pieces

10 sweet mini peppers, assorted colors

2 Italian long hot peppers, sliced

2 onions, peeled and sliced

1 tbsp. tomato paste

1 tsp. oregano

1 tsp. basil

1 tsp. salt

1 tsp. ground black pepper

Directions

1. Place the Copper Chef on high heat. Add 2 tbsp. olive oil.

2. Sear all of the sweet and hot sausage.

3. Cover and lower heat to medium. Cook for 10 minutes. Remove sausage and set aside.

4. Add the rest of the olive oil. Sauté the mini peppers, onions, tomato paste, herbs, salt, and black pepper on high heat for about 5 minutes.

5. Slice the sausage, then return it to the Copper Chef with the peppers and onions. Cook for 10 additional minutes on low heat before serving.

Eric's Tip: You can also make a lighter version using poultry sausage. I love this served over rice or pasta. This also makes a delicious sandwich on ciabatta with sharp provolone.

Ingredients

4 (6 oz.) tilapia fillets

3 eggs

salt and pepper

dusting flour

4 tbsp. olive oil

1 fresh lemon, half for juice, half cut into slices

1/3 cup white wine

1/2 cup fish broth

1/4 cup fresh Italian parsley, chopped

2 tbsp. capers

2 tbsp. butter

Tilapia Francese

Directions

1. Beat eggs, salt, and pepper in a mixing bowl until light and frothy.

2. Lightly dust tilapia with flour and shake off excess.

3. Place the Copper Chef on high heat. When the pan is hot, add the olive oil.

4. Dip tilapia fillets in egg wash. Place fillets in the Copper Chef.

5. Cook tilapia fillets for 2 minutes on each side. Remove from pan and plate.

6. Degrease pan. Add lemon slices, white wine, and lemon juice to the pan. Use a wooden spoon to scrape the pan.

7. Add fish broth, capers, and parsley. Simmer for 2 minutes.

8. Remove Copper Chef from heat. Stir in butter.

9. Pour sauce over tilapia before serving.

Eric's Tip: If fresh tilapia is not available, most supermarkets carry IQF (individually quick frozen) tilapia in the freezer section. It's extremely convenient and the quality is great. Just thaw according to directions.

Pan-Seared Tuna with Mango Pineapple Salsa

SERVES 4

Ingredients

4 (4-6 oz.) tuna steaks

2 tbsp. olive oil

3 tbsp. Montreal steak seasoning

1 tbsp. fresh lemon juice

1 tbsp. olive oil, for searing

Salsa:

1½ cups ripe mango, diced

1½ cups ripe pineapple, diced

½ cup cucumber, peeled, seeded and diced

3 tbsp. red onion, diced

1 scallion, chopped

2 tbsp. rice vinegar

1 tbsp. honey

1 tsp. cumin

¼ cup red bell pepper, diced

¼ cup fresh cilantro, chopped

1 jalapeño pepper, seeds removed and diced

Directions

1. Marinate tuna steaks in olive oil, lemon juice, and Montreal seasoning for 15 minutes.

2. In a medium bowl, combine all salsa ingredients. Mix well and refrigerate.

3. Place the Copper Chef on high heat. When the pan is hot, add the olive oil. Sear the tuna steaks for 2-4 minutes per side until desired doneness.

Eric's Tip: Tuna tastes the best cooked rare, but you should cook it however you like it. It tends to become dry when cooked all the way through. This recipe is great with any fish or even with scallops and shrimp.

Ingredients

2 lb. salmon, skinless and boneless

4 tbsp. chives, chopped

2 tbsp. basil, chopped

1 tbsp. Dijon mustard

1 clove garlic, minced

salt and pepper

1 egg white

Salmon Burgers

Directions

1. Rough chop salmon and place in a food processor. Pulse 10-15 times for a smooth texture, then transfer to a mixing bowl.

2. Add chives, basil, Dijon, garlic, egg white, salt, and pepper. Mix well. Portion into 6 patties. Refrigerate for 15 minutes.

3. Place the Copper Chef on medium-high heat. When the pan is hot, add the olive oil. Sauté for 3-5 minutes per side before serving.

Eric's Tip: You can make these 8 smaller burgers, or, if you prefer, you can make 4 large burgers and they will all fit into the Copper Chef at the same time. The larger burgers will need more time to cook.

Flounder in Saffron Tomato Broth

SERVES 4

Ingredients

3 tbsp. olive oil

1 cup sweet potato, ¼-inch diced

½ cup carrots, ½-inch diced

½ cup onion, chopped

2 cloves garlic, smashed

1 tsp. saffron

1 tsp. fennel seed

⅓ cup white wine

2½ cups clam broth

1 (12 oz.) can of chopped tomatoes

3 tbsp. basil, chiffonade (see tip)

salt and pepper

4 (4-6 oz.) flounder fillets

Directions

1. Place the Copper Chef on medium-high heat. When the pan is hot, add olive oil. Add sweet potato, carrot, and onion. Sweat on medium-high heat for 8-10 minutes.

2. Add garlic, saffron, fennel seed, and white wine. Cook for 3 minutes.

3. Add clam broth, chopped tomatoes, basil, salt, and pepper. Reduce to a simmer.

4. Gently tuck flounder fillets into the broth. Cover and simmer for 8-10 minutes until done.

Eric's Tip: "Chiffonade" is a cutting technique in which you stack the leaves and roll them tightly. You then make perpendicular cuts to create thin strips.

Prosciutto-Wrapped Cod with Edamame Salad

SERVES 4

Ingredients

3 cups edamame, shelled

1 clove garlic, chopped

¼ tsp. chili flakes

3 tbsp. olive oil

2 tbsp. fresh basil, chopped

1 fresh lemon, juice and zest

2 tbsp. grated Parmesan cheese

salt and pepper

2 oz. Prosciutto (4-6 slices)

3 tbsp. olive oil, to sauté cod

4 (6 oz.) cod fillets

Directions

1. Combine edamame, garlic, chili flakes, olive oil, basil, lemon juice, lemon zest, Parmesan cheese, salt, and pepper. Mix well and refrigerate.

2. Wrap cod fillets with 1 or 2 pieces of prosciutto.

3. Place the Copper Chef on medium-high heat. When the pan is hot, add the olive oil.

4. Sauté cod for 3-5 minutes per side.

5. Serve with edamame salad.

Eric's Tip: The great thing about the edamame salad is that it's even better when it's prepared the day before and left to sit overnight. You can also substitute any kind of bean that you want; I prefer cannellini or a nice big butter bean.

Ingredients

¼ cup extra virgin olive oil

1 onion, peeled and minced

6 cloves garlic, peeled and minced

24 clams, Littleneck

2 cups chopped clams, with juice

¼ cup white wine

¼ cup chopped parsley

1 tsp. crushed red pepper

1 tsp. sea salt

¾ lb. fusilli pasta, cooked and tossed in 3 tbsp. butter

Fusilli and Clams

Directions

1. Place the Copper Chef on medium-high heat. Add olive oil, onion, and garlic. Cook for about 4 minutes until the onions are translucent.

2. Add the clams (in-shell), juice from the chopped clams, and white wine. Cover.Cook until the clams open.

3. Add the chopped clams, parsley, crushed red pepper, sea salt, and fusilli pasta, stir. Cover and cook for about 4 minutes before serving.

Eric's Tip: If you don't have access to fresh clams, simply double the amount of chopped clams. Stores occasionally sell cooked frozen clams (in-shell) in the freezer section. They work great as well!

Linguini Carbonara

Ingredients

1 lb. linguini

2 tbsp. olive oil

1 lb. bacon, diced

½ onion, peeled and diced

2 cloves of garlic minced

1 cup grated Parmesan cheese

4 egg yolks

2 tbsp. parsley, chopped

½ tsp. ground black pepper

½ tsp. sea salt

Directions

1. Cook the linguini in the Copper Chef, reserving ½ cup of the pasta water when draining. Set pasta aside.

2. Place the Copper Chef on medium-high heat. When the pan is hot, add the olive oil and the bacon. Cook until almost cooked through, then add the onions and garlic. Sauté until the onions are translucent, careful not to burn the garlic.

3. In a bowl, mix together the egg yolks, parsley, Parmesan cheese, sea salt, and black pepper.

4. On medium heat, toss the cooked linguini into the onions and bacon until the pasta is warmed. Add the reserved pasta water and toss until incorporated.

5. Turn off the heat.

6. Immediately pour the egg mixture into the pan. Toss until well incorporated.

7. Serve immediately.

Eric's Tip: My favorite way to make this is with a pound of chopped speck (a type of dried pork) instead of classic bacon. My supermarket carries it all of the time. To try a variation on this classic recipe, give speck a try.

Ingredients

1 lb. cooked penne pasta

3 tbsp. olive oil

½ onion, peeled and minced

3 cloves garlic, peeled and minced

¼ cup vodka

¾ cup crushed tomato

1 tsp. oregano, dried

2 tsp. basil, dried

1 qt. heavy cream

½ tsp. sea salt

½ tsp. ground black pepper

Penne alla Vodka

Directions

1. Place the Copper Chef on medium-high heat. When the pan is hot, add the olive oil. Sauté the onions and garlic until slightly golden.

2. Add the vodka, tomatoes, oregano, and basil. Cook for 4 minutes.

3. Add the cream. Bring to a boil and then reduce the sauce until slightly thickened.

4. Reduce heat to a simmer. Add the pasta, sea salt, and black pepper. Cook until the pasta is hot and coated well.

5. Serve.

Eric's Tip: When cooking with any wine, beer or liquor, always cook with what you like to drink. If you don't like to drink it, you won't like it in your recipe, either!

Eric's
Braised Creations

Meatballs and Sunday Gravy

Swedish Meatballs

Veal and Peppers

Coq Au Vin

Chicken Cacciatore

Chicken and Dumplings

Green Chile Pork

**Braised Pork Shoulder
with Browned Sauerkraut**

Pork Osso Buco

Braised Pork Shoulder

Beef Stew

Pork Braciole

Braised Lamb Shanks

Lamb Stew

**Wiener Schnitzel
with Braised Red Cabbage**

Braising is a technique where you use high heat to sear the main ingredient and then low heat and a lid to finish the cooking. The Copper Chef excels at braising because you can braise on the stovetop or in the oven using it. The lid has a large metal handle, which allows it to go into the oven easily. It gives you a nice space to use your oven mitt to take the lid off to check your food's progress in the oven. If you have a recipe that calls for braising on the stove, give it a try in the oven or vice versa. It's nice to have options!

Meatballs and Sunday Gravy

Ingredients

Meatballs:

4 lb. ground beef

3 cloves garlic, peeled and minced

½ onion, peeled and minced

¼ cup parsley, chopped

½ cup Parmesan cheese, grated

1 cup breadcrumbs

⅓ cup milk

4 eggs

1 tsp. sea salt

½ tsp. ground black pepper

Gravy:

4 tbsp. olive oil, for searing

½ lb. pork country ribs, bone-in

1 onion, peeled and diced

4 cloves garlic, peeled and minced

2 (25 oz.) cans crushed tomatoes

½ cup Parmesan cheese, grated

½ cup red wine

1 tsp. sea salt

1 tsp. ground black pepper

1 tsp. oregano, dried

1 tbsp. basil, dried

1 large carrot

10 basil leaves, fresh, chopped

¼ cup parsley, chopped for garnish

Directions

1. Place the ground beef and all the meatball ingredients in a bowl. Mix well.

2. Form the meatballs.

3. Place the Copper Chef on medium-high heat. When the pan is hot, add olive oil. Sear the pork ribs, then add the onion and garlic. Sauté until the onions are translucent, being careful not to burn the garlic.

4. Add the tomatoes, Parmesan cheese, dried herbs, red wine, sea salt, and black pepper. Stir well.

5. Bring to a boil, stirring constantly. Once the gravy has boiled, reduce to a simmer.

6. Add the meatballs to the gravy. Drop in the whole carrot. Simmer on low for 1½-2 hours.

7. Remove the carrot. Add the fresh basil. Serve with pasta and garnish with parsley.

Eric's Tip: I don't brown my meatballs before adding them to my gravy. This makes for a softer meatball. If you prefer firmer meatballs, feel free to sear them before adding to the gravy. The carrot is included to add a little bit of sweetness (but not too much).

SERVES 6-8

Ingredients

2 lb. ground beef

1 cup breadcrumbs, plain

4 eggs

2 tbsp. Worcestershire sauce

1 tsp. sea salt

½ tsp. ground black pepper

½ onion, peeled and minced

½ cup heavy cream

1 tsp. allspice

3 tbsp. olive oil

Sauce:

¼ cup butter

1 tsp. shallots, peeled and minced

¼ cup flour, all purpose

5 cups beef stock

¼ cup heavy cream

Swedish Meatballs

Directions

1. In a large bowl, mix the ground beef, breadcrumbs, eggs, Worcestershire sauce, sea salt, black pepper, onion, ½ cup heavy cream, and allspice. Mix well. Roll into small meatballs.

2. Preheat the Copper Chef pan on the stovetop on medium heat. Add olive oil.

3. Sear the meatballs in batches.

4. When all of the meatballs are seared, drain the oil from the pan.

5. Make the sauce: place the Copper Chef on medium heat. Add butter. Sauté the shallots for 3 minutes or until translucent. Stir or whisk in flour. Cook for 5 minutes on low.

6. Slowly add the beef stock, whisking to incorporate. Once the sauce is boiling, bring to a simmer. Add the meatballs.

7. Simmer. After 30 minutes, add the rest of the heavy cream.

8. Stir and serve.

Eric's Tip: Swedish meatballs aren't just for egg noodles. Try turning them into a delicious slider or sub with sautéed cabbage spiked with caraway seed.

Veal and Peppers

Ingredients

3 tbsp. olive oil

3 lb. veal, cubed

1 red pepper, seeded and diced

1 green bell pepper, seeded and diced

1 onion, peeled and diced

2 cloves garlic, peeled and minced

¼ cup red wine

1 (25 oz.) can crushed tomatoes

¼ cup parsley

1 bay leaf

2 sprigs thyme

1 tsp. sea salt

½ tsp. ground black pepper

Directions

1. Place the Copper Chef on high heat. When the pan is hot, add the olive oil. Sauté the veal until golden.

2. Add the onions, garlic, red and green peppers. Stir. Cook until tender, about 5-8 minutes.

3. Pour in the red wine, tomatoes, parsley, bay leaf, thyme, sea salt, and black pepper.

4. Cover. Reduce heat to a simmer and cook for about 45 minutes until the veal is tender.

5. Serve.

Eric's Tip: This recipe also works great with cubed chicken or pork.

SERVES 4-6

Ingredients

6-8 pieces chicken, legs and thighs

salt and pepper

¼ cup flour

4 strips of bacon, sliced

2 cups frozen pearl onions, thawed

¾ lb. cremini mushrooms, sliced

½ cup carrot, diced

½ cup celery, diced

2 cups red wine

1 cup chicken stock

2 cloves garlic, crushed

2 tsp. Herbes de Provence

1 bay leaf

¼ cup fresh Italian parsley, chopped

Coq Au Vin

Directions

1. Season chicken with salt and pepper. Lightly dust chicken with flour, shaking off any excess.

2. Place the Copper Chef on medium heat. Add bacon and sauté until crispy. Remove to a paper towel.

3. In the Copper Chef, sear chicken for 8-10 minutes until brown. Remove and set aside.

4. Add onions, carrot, celery, and mushrooms. Sauté for 5 minutes, then add garlic.

5. Deglaze pan with red wine.

6. Add chicken stock, bay leaf, Herbes de Provence, bacon, and chicken.

7. Bring to a boil, then reduce to a simmer. Cover with lid for 35 minutes.

8. Remove lid. Continue to simmer for another 25 minutes to let sauce thicken.

9. Stir in parsley before serving.

Eric's Tip: This recipe was made famous in the 1960s by Julia Child. My version gives you amazing flavor without the traditional overnight marinade.

Ingredients

6-8 pieces chicken legs and thighs, skinless

salt and pepper

3 tbsp. olive oil

1 green bell pepper, sliced

1 cup yellow onion, sliced

1 oz. dried porcini mushrooms, reconstituted in 1 cup water

2 cloves garlic, smashed

½ cup red wine

1 tbsp. tomato paste

1 (14 oz. can) crushed tomatoes

1 tsp. dry oregano

½ tsp. red chili flakes

1 cup chicken stock

6 leaves fresh basil

Chicken Cacciatore

Directions

1. Preheat the oven to 375° F.

2. Season chicken with salt and pepper. Heat olive oil in the Copper Chef pan.

3. Brown chicken for 5-8 minutes, then remove. Degrease the pan.

4. Add green pepper and onion. Sauté. After 5 minutes, add mushrooms, garlic, and tomato paste.

5. Deglaze with red wine. Add crushed tomatos, oregano, red chili flakes, chicken stock, and fresh basil.

6. Return chicken to the pan.

7. Cook uncovered in the oven for 30-40 minutes, stirring occasionally.

8. Serve.

Eric's Tip: If you can't find dried porcini mushrooms, add in ¼ cup of sweet sherry to get that rich flavor. I love shredding the leftover chicken in the sauce and serving it over pasta or rice the next day.

Ingredients

2 boneless chicken breasts, skinless and cut into bite-sized pieces

4 boneless chicken thighs, skinless and cut into bite-sized pieces

2 cups chicken stock

1 (10.5 oz) can beef consommé

1 large onion, peeled and diced

2 stalks celery, diced

2 sprigs thyme

1 sprig marjoram

1 bay leaf

3 tbsp. butter

3 tbsp. flour

2 tbsp. parsley, chopped

½ tsp. sea salt

½ tsp. ground black pepper

Dumplings:

1½ cups flour

2 tbsp. butter

½ tsp. sea salt

2 tsp. baking powder

1 egg

¼ cup milk

Chicken and Dumplings

Directions

1. Place the Copper Chef on medium-high heat. Add the chicken, chicken stock, beef consommé, onion, celery, thyme, marjoram, and bay leaf. Cover.

2. In a small bowl, mix together the butter and flour. When the chicken is boiling, stir in the flour and butter mixture. Cook for 45 minutes on a high simmer. Cover.

3. Make the dumplings: in a bowl, mix together the flour, sea salt, baking powder, and butter to make pea size crumbs. Add the egg and milk. Mix.

4. After 45 minutes, uncover the chicken and season with sea salt, black pepper, and chopped parsley.

5. With a tablespoon, spoon the dumplings onto the top. Cook for about 10 more minutes before serving.

Eric's Tip: No time to make dumplings? Buy a can of refrigerated biscuits and cut each into fours. Use these to top the dish instead of homemade dumplings.

Ingredients

3 tbsp. olive oil

1 lb. tomatillos, quartered

1 jalapeño pepper

3 cloves garlic

1 medium onion, ½ inch sliced

2 tbsp. olive oil, to brown ribs

2 lb. boneless pork country ribs

2 cups beef stock

1 tbsp. ground cumin

⅓ cup fresh cilantro, chopped

salt and pepper

Green Chile Pork

Directions

1. Preheat the oven to 425° F.

2. Toss tomatillos, jalapeño, garlic, and onion in olive oil. In the Copper Chef pan, roast onion mixture in the oven for 20-25 minutes. Let cool, then purée in a food processor.

3. Place the Copper Chef on high heat. Add the oil. Brown the pork for 12-15 minutes.

4. Add vegetable purée, beef stock, and cumin. Stir.

5. Reduce heat to medium-low. Simmer for 40-50 minutes.

6. During the last 5 minutes of cooking, add chopped cilantro. Adjust seasoning with salt and pepper before serving.

Eric's Tip: If tomatillos are not available, add in 1½ cups of salsa verde.

Braised Pork Shoulder with Browned Sauerkraut

SERVES 4-6

Ingredients

2 ½ - 3 lb. boneless pork shoulder, cut in four sections

salt and pepper

3 tbsp. olive oil

1 cup white onion, chopped

1 cup carrot, chopped

1 cup celery, chopped

3 cloves garlic, smashed

1 cup white wine

2 cups beef stock

2 tsp. fennel seed

2 tsp. dry oregano

Sauerkraut:

16 oz. quality sauerkraut, drained

2 tbsp. olive oil

¼ lb. bacon, diced

salt and pepper

Directions

1. Preheat the oven to 325° F.

2. Season pork with salt and pepper.

3. Place the Copper Chef on high heat. When the pan is hot, add the olive oil. Sear pork until deep brown on all sides. Remove from pan and set aside.

4. Add onion, carrot, celery, and garlic. Sauté for 6-8 minutes.

5. Deglaze with white wine.

6. Add beef stock, fennel seed, oregano, and pork.

7. Bring stock to a boil. Cover and place in the oven for about 2 hours or until tender.

8. When the pork is done, transfer to a bowl and set aside.

For the sauerkraut:

9. Place the cleaned Copper Chef on medium heat. When the pan is hot, add the olive oil and diced bacon. Cook until golden brown.

10. Add sauerkraut and the sauce from the pork shoulder. Cook on medium-low heat. Stir often so that it does not burn, about 45 minutes.

11. If the sauerkraut starts to dry up, add some water to keep it from burning.

12. Season pork with salt and pepper, to taste. Slice and serve with the sauerkraut.

Eric's Tip: This recipe takes a while, but if you have the time, it's one of my favorites.

Ingredients

3½ lb. pork shanks

salt and pepper

½ cup flour

4 tbsp. olive oil

1 cup yellow onion, chopped

½ cup celery, diced

½ cup carrot, diced

2 cloves garlic, smashed

3 tbsp. tomato paste

2 cups red wine

1 qt. beef stock

2 bay leaves

zest of one fresh orange

zest of one fresh lemon

¼ cup fresh Italian parsley, chopped, for garnish

Pork Osso Buco

Directions

1. Preheat the oven to 375° F.

2. Season pork shanks with salt and pepper. Dust with flour.

3. Place the Copper Chef on high heat. Once hot, add the olive oil. Sear pork shanks until you achieve a nice, deep brown color. Remove and set aside.

4. Add onion, carrot, and celery. Sauté for about 5 minutes until soft.

5. Add tomato paste and garlic. Cook for another minute.

6. Add red wine to deglaze. Cook for 3 minutes. Add the beef stock, bay leaves, and citrus zest. Return pork shanks to the Copper Chef. Cover with the lid.

7. Cook in the oven for 1 hour at 375° F. Remove lid, then reduce heat to 325° F. Cook for 30 minutes, basting frequently.

8. Plate. Garnish with parsley before serving.

Eric's Tip: This is a great twist on an old recipe. Traditionally, this dish is made with veal shanks, but they are more expensive and harder to find. Using the pork, you can keep the same flavor profile and save some cash for dessert!

SERVES 4-6

Ingredients

2 ½ -3 lb. boneless pork shoulder, cut in four sections

3 tbsp. olive oil

1 cup white onion, chopped

1 cup carrot, chopped

1 cup celery, chopped

3 cloves garlic, smashed

1 cup white wine

2 cups beef stock

2 tsp. fennel seed

2 tsp. dry oregano

salt and pepper

Braised Pork Shoulder

Directions

1. Preheat the oven to 325° F. Season pork with salt and pepper.

2. Place the Copper Chef on high heat. Add olive oil. Sear the pork for 8-10 minutes until deep brown. Remove from pan and set aside.

3. Add onion, carrot, celery, and garlic. Sauté for 6-8 minutes.

4. Deglaze pan with white wine.

5. Add beef stock, fennel seed, oregano, and pork.

6. Bring stock to a boil. Cover. Place in the oven for 1½ -2 hours or until tender.

7. Serve

Eric's Tip: As the shoulder is resting, skim the fat off the braising liquid and thicken the liquid with ½ cup instant potato flakes. As I'm simmering this gravy, I mash the vegetables in the pan to optimize flavor. Strain, then enjoy!

Ingredients

3 lb. beef, top round, cubed

salt and pepper, to season beef

2 cups flour

3 tbsp. olive oil

2 cloves garlic, peeled and minced

1 onion, peeled and diced

2 stalks celery, diced

2 carrots, peeled and diced

10 baby potatoes, quartered

1 cup beer, amber

⅛ cup balsamic vinegar

3 cups beef stock

1 bay leaf

2 sprigs thyme

1 sprig rosemary

½ tsp. sea salt

½ tsp. ground black pepper

1 cup peas, frozen

Beef Stew

Directions

1. Place the Copper Chef pan on high heat. When the pan is hot, add the olive oil.

2. Salt and pepper the beef. Dust the meat with flour. Brown in the Copper Chef.

3. Add the garlic and sauté for 3 minutes. Add the rest of the ingredients except the peas.

4. Cover. Lower the heat and simmer for about 1-1½ hours.

5. After one hour of cooking, add the peas.

6. Serve when meat is tender.

Eric's Tip: To give this recipe a different flavor profile, you can substitute a dry red wine for the amber beer.

Ingredients

1 lb. chopped frozen spinach, thawed and squeezed dry

4 tbsp. toasted pine nuts

¼ tbsp. raisins

1 hard-boiled egg, chopped

⅓ cup Parmesan cheese, grated

1 clove garlic, chopped

3 tbsp. olive oil

8 (4 oz.) boneless pork chops, pounded thin

½ cup red wine

1 jar marinara sauce

1 cup water

Pork Braciole

Directions

1. Combine spinach, pine nuts, raisins, chopped hard-boiled egg, Parmesan cheese, and garlic. Mix well.

2. Lay pork out. Distribute spinach mixture evenly on top.

3. Roll, filling tightly and tucking sides in like a burrito. You can use toothpicks to secure.

4. Place the Copper Chef on high heat, then add the olive oil. Brown rolled pork for 5-8 minutes.

5. Drain excess grease and deglaze the pan with red wine.

6. Add marinara sauce and water. Stir. Cover and reduce heat to medium-low. Simmer for 45-60 minutes.

Eric's Tip: These make great party sandwiches. If you are in the mood for something other than hoagies for your Sunday sports party, slice each braciole in half and place into a slider bun.

Ingredients

4 lamb shanks

3 tbsp. olive oil

1 tsp. sea salt

1 tsp. ground black pepper

1 onion, peeled and minced

2 cloves garlic, peeled and minced

2 shallots, peeled and minced

1 stalk celery, small diced

1 large carrot, peeled and small diced

2 tbsp. tomato paste

1 cup red wine

2 cups beef stock

zest of one lemon

1 sprig rosemary

1 bay leaf

Braised Lamb Shanks

Directions

1. Preheat the oven to 375° F.

2. Place the Copper Chef on high heat. When the pan is hot, add the olive oil. Season the lamb shanks with sea salt and black pepper. Sear on all sides.

3. Remove the shanks from the pan. Set aside. Add garlic, shallots, celery, and carrot. Sauté for 3-4 minutes.

4. Add the tomato paste and cook for another 3 minutes. Deglaze the Copper Chef with red wine. Add the beef stock, lemon zest, rosemary, and bay leaf. Return lamb shanks back to the Copper Chef. Cover.

5. Put the Copper Chef in the oven. Cook for 1½-2 hours until the meat falls off the bone.

6. Serve.

Eric's Tip: A great variation is to use pork shanks instead of lamb. Either way, I like it with some finely-chopped mint added at the very end.

Ingredients

2 lb. boneless leg of lamb, cubed

2 cups flour, for dusting

3 tbsp. olive oil

4 cloves garlic, peeled and minced

2 tbsp. tomato paste

1 tsp. dry thyme

1 cup beef stock

½ can Guinness beer

3 shakes of Worcestershire sauce

10 pearl onions, peeled

8 baby red potatoes, cut in halves

8 baby carrots, cut in halves

1 sprig rosemary

1 bay leaf

1 cup cooked peas

2 tbsp. orange zest

½ cup fresh chopped mint, for garnish

sea salt & freshly ground pepper, to taste

Lamb Stew

Directions

1. Place the Copper Chef on high heat. When the pan is hot, add the olive oil.

2. Dust the lamb with flour. Brown in the Copper Chef.

3. Add the garlic and tomato paste. Sauté for 3 minutes. Add the rest of the ingredients except the peas. Stir. Simmer with the lid on for about 1-1½ hours.

4. After 1 hour of cooking, add the peas.

5. When the meat is tender, serve.

Wiener Schnitzel with Braised Red Cabbage

Ingredients

1 lb. red cabbage, shredded

1 Granny Smith apple, diced

3 tbsp. olive oil

¼ cup red wine vinegar

½ cup apple cider

⅛ tsp. allspice

2 tbsp. brown sugar

8 (4 oz.) veal cutlets

½ cup flour

2 eggs, beaten

1½ cups breadcrumbs, plain

¼ tsp. fresh ground nutmeg

salt and pepper

2 tbsp. butter

2 tbsp. olive oil, to cook cutlets

Directions

1. Place the Copper Chef on medium heat. Add olive oil, red cabbage, and diced Granny Smith apple. Sweat for 10-15 minutes.

2. Add vinegar, brown sugar, allspice, and apple cider. Simmer on low for 25-30 minutes, or until all the liquid is reduced to a glaze.

3. When the cabbage is done, set aside in a dish.

4. If cutlets are a little thick, place between two pieces of plastic film and pound to ¼-inch thick.

5. Season veal with salt and pepper.

6. In a separate bowl, combine flour and nutmeg. Dust cutlets with flour and nutmeg mixture, shaking off excess. Dip in egg, then coat with breadcrumbs.

7. Place the Copper Chef on medium-high heat. Add the butter and olive oil, being careful not to burn the butter. Cook cutlets on each side for 2-3 minutes until cooked through. Hold in a 150º F oven on a baking rack until ready to serve.

Eric's Tip: "Schnitzel" is basically a generic term for a breaded cutlet of meat, so you can substitute any type of meat and still get great results. My favorite variation is the German style that uses a breaded pork cutlet topped with a delicious mushroom gravy and a side of spaetzle.

Savory
Baked Meals

Shepherd's Pie

Beef Enchiladas

Chicken Parm

Chicken Pot Pie

Sausage Frittata

Stuffed Pork Medallions

Pineapple-Glazed Ham

Teriyaki Pork Tenderloins

Quiche Lorraine

Giant Frittata

Bleu Cheese Stuffed Mushrooms

Lime Cilantro Seafood Bake

Eggplant Parmesan

Au Gratin Potatoes

Spaghetti Pie

Sweet Potatoes
with Marshmallows

Baked Ziti

Noodle Kugel

Vegetable Lasagna

We designed the Copper Chef with metal handles and high heat-resistance so you can put the pan into the oven. This allows you to bake everything from a giant frittata to a shepherd's pie in your Copper Chef! The Copper Chef has an amazing ceramic nonstick coating that allows food to slide out so nicely without sticking. In fact, with the square sides being slightly sloped, foods release even easier than they would in a traditional square baker. Since the nonstick can take heat up to 850° F, you even get the flexibility to use the broiler feature to brown the top of your food or melt some cheese on top!

Ingredients

Serves 4-6

3 tbsp. olive oil

1 cup onion, chopped

1 cup carrot, chopped

1 cup turnips, chopped

1 lb. lean ground beef

1 tbsp. tomato paste

1 cup beef stock

2 tbsp. flour

¾ cup frozen peas

¾ cup frozen corn

1 tbsp. Worcestershire sauce

1 tsp. dry thyme

salt and pepper

4 cups prepared mashed yams

1 egg

Shepherd's Pie

Directions

1. Preheat the oven to 350° F.

2. Place the Copper Chef on medium heat. Add olive oil, ground beef, onion, carrot, and turnips. Cook for 10-12 minutes. Drain any excess fat.

3. Add tomato paste. Cook for 2 more minutes.

4. Add flour, beef stock, Worcestershire sauce, thyme, peas, and corn. Stir. Simmer for 10 minutes until sauce thickens. Pour into the Copper Chef.

5. In a separate bowl, combine mashed yams and egg. Mix well. Spread on top of the beef mixture.

6. Place Copper Chef into the oven. Cook for 30 minutes on 350° F.

7. Season with salt and pepper before serving.

Eric's Tip: I like this with sweet potatoes or yams, but you can easily swap it out and use regular mashed potatoes.

Ingredients

2 tbsp. olive oil

1 lb. lean ground beef

1 cup onion, chopped

2 tsp. fresh garlic cloves, chopped

1 tbsp. chili powder

1 tsp. cumin

½ tsp. coriander

½ tsp. salt

½ tsp. black pepper

1 cup salsa

2 (10 oz. cans) enchilada or Mexican red sauce

2 cups Mexican blend cheese, shredded

1 tbsp. fresh cilantro, chopped

8 (6.5") flour tortillas

Beef Enchiladas

Directions

1. Preheat the oven to 325° F.

2. Season the ground beef with salt and black pepper. Place the Copper Chef on medium-high heat. Add olive oil. When the olive oil is hot, brown the ground beef. Drain excess fat and set aside.

3. Add onions and garlic to the pan. Cook until translucent. Be careful not to burn the garlic.

4. Add chili powder, cumin, coriander, salt, and black pepper. Cook for about a minute.

5. Add the browned beef and salsa. Stir well. Place the lid on the Copper Chef and let simmer on medium-low for 20 minutes, stirring occasionally.

6. Pour mixture into a large bowl. Set aside.

7. Pour about ½ cup of the enchilada sauce into the Copper Chef. Spread evenly on the bottom of the pan.

8. Warm the tortillas slightly. Spoon beef mixture onto each tortilla. Do not overfill so that you can still roll the enchilada.

9. Place 4 enchiladas on the bottom of the Copper Chef. Top with half of the cheese and more enchilada sauce. Repeat with remaining enchiladas.

10. Place in the oven and cook for about 15 minutes or until hot.

11. Garnish with fresh chopped cilantro before serving.

Eric's Tip: Transform into breakfast burritos by scrambling an egg into the leftover ground beef mix. Remember to top with sour cream.

SERVES 2

Ingredients

2 chicken breasts, skinless

½ tsp. salt

1 tsp. ground black pepper

½ cup flour

1 egg

2 tbsp. milk

1 cup seasoned breadcrumbs

½ tsp. sea salt

1 tsp. ground black pepper

½ tsp. onion powder

½ tsp. garlic powder

1 tbsp. parsley, chopped

½ tsp. oregano, dry

2 tbsp. Parmesan cheese, grated, for breadcrumb mixture

½ cup olive oil

2 cups tomato sauce

4 thick slices mozzarella

¼ cup Parmesan cheese, grated, for topping

Chicken Parm

Directions

1. Preheat the oven to 375° F.

2. Season the chicken breasts with sea salt and black pepper. Put the chicken between two sheets of plastic wrap. Pound using a mallet or the bottom of a pan.

3. Place the flour in a flat pan or large bowl for dusting the chicken.

4. In another bowl, mix the egg and milk. In another flat pan or bowl, mix the breadcrumbs with the spices, herbs, and 2 tbsp. grated Parmesan cheese.

5. Dip the chicken in the flour, then into the egg mixture, and finally into the breadcrumbs. Shake off excess.

6. Place the Copper Chef on medium-high heat. When the pan is hot, add olive oil. Cook the breaded chicken until golden on each side. Set aside.

7. In a clean Copper Chef, pour 1 cup tomato sauce. Add chicken, top with more sauce and both the mozzarella and grated cheeses.

8. Place into the oven. Cook for about 15 minutes or until the sauce and cheese are hot.

Eric's Tip: Most people serve this with spaghetti, but it's also great served with rice.

SERVES 10

Ingredients

1 stick butter

1 cup frozen pearl onions

2 stalks celery, cut into 2" pieces

1/3 cup flour

4 cups chicken stock

14 chicken tenders, raw, cut in half

1½ cups baby carrots

10 baby potatoes

1 bay leaf

1 sprig marjoram

½ tsp. turmeric

¼ cup heavy cream plus 1 tbsp. for finish

1 cup frozen peas

4 pie crusts

Chicken Pot Pie

Directions

1. Preheat the oven to 375° F.

2. Place the Copper Chef on medium-high heat. Cook butter, onions, and celery for 4 minutes. Stir in the flour. Cook for about two minutes.

3. Slowly add the chicken stock. Whisk to incorporate the flour and butter for a smooth, silky sauce.

4. Add the chicken, carrots, potatoes, bay leaf, marjoram, and turmeric. Bring to a boil. Cook for 15 minutes on simmer. Add the heavy cream and peas. Stir. Let thicken for a few minutes, then turn off the heat.

5. Remove filling from the pan. Set aside to cool.

6. In a clean Copper Chef, drape 3 pie shells on the bottom and sides.

7. Pour the chicken and potatoes into the Copper Chef. Place the 4th pie shell on top. Fold in all the sides of the other pie shells from the bottom of the pan.

8. Make a couple of slits in the top of the pie.

9. Brush the top of the pie with heavy cream. Place the pan into the oven.

10. Cook until the pie crust is nice and golden.

11. Let cool before serving.

Eric's Tip: When I'm short on time, I skip the pie crust lining. Instead, I use puff pastry (from the freezer section) on top for a fun, fast variation my kids love.

Ingredients

3 tbsp. olive oil

2 lb. Italian sausage (hot or sweet)

3 cups potatoes, diced and blanched

2 cups red and green bell peppers, seeded and diced

1 cup onions, peeled and diced

1 cup scallions, chopped

1 tbsp. sea salt

1 tbsp. ground black pepper

6 cups eggs, beaten

½ cup milk

1 cup fresh tomatoes, diced

1 cup feta, crumbled

Sausage Frittata

Directions

1. Preheat the oven to 350° F.

2. Place the Copper Chef on medium-high heat. When the pan is hot, add the olive oil and brown the sausage.

3. Add the potatoes and brown lightly. Add the peppers and onions. Cook with lid on for about 5 minutes.

4. Reserve diced tomatoes and feta. Add the rest of the ingredients. Stir. Place the pan into the oven. Cook about 1½ hours or until the eggs are firm.

5. Top with diced tomatoes and feta before serving.

Eric's Tip: Short on time? You can always substitute frozen hash browns from the freezer section for the blanched potatoes.

Ingredients

2 tbsp. butter

1 onion, small diced

½ celery stalk, small diced

½ carrot, peeled and diced small

6 mushrooms, chopped

½ red pepper, diced small

1 cup bread, cubed

¼ cup chicken stock

1 sprig tarragon, chopped

1 sprig thyme, leaves removed and chopped

½ tsp. sea salt

½ tsp. ground black pepper

3 tbsp. olive oil

4 pork medallions

Sauce:

2 tbsp. butter

1 shallot, peeled and minced

2 sprigs tarragon

½ cup white wine

1½ cups chicken stock

¼ cup cream

¼ tsp. salt

¼ tsp. ground black pepper

Stuffed Pork Medallions

Directions

1. Preheat the oven to 375° F.

2. Place the Copper Chef on medium-high heat. Melt the butter. Sweat the onions, celery, carrots, mushrooms, and peppers until tender. Add the herbs, sea salt, and black pepper.

3. Add the cubed bread and chicken stock. Stir. Remove mixture from Copper Chef and set aside to cool.

4. Slice the pork medallions lengthwise to make a pocket. Stuff with the filling.

5. Place a clean Copper Chef on medium heat. When the pan is hot, add olive oil. Sear the medallions on both sides. Place the Copper Chef into the oven. Cook for about 20 minutes or until internal temperature is 160° F.

6. Remove Copper Chef from the oven. Set aside to rest for 10 minutes.

7. Place the Copper Chef on medium heat. When the pan is hot, add the butter and shallot. Cook for 2 minutes. Add the wine and stock with the herbs. Bring to a boil. When the sauce has reduced by about 1/3, add the cream. Cook for another 3-4 minutes, stirring often. Season with sea salt and black pepper.

8. Serve the pork medallions with the sauce.

Eric's Tip: For a fast(er) variation, pan-sear the medallions and add a bit of mustard to the sauce for an easy, bistro-style dish.

Ingredients

½ cup brown sugar

2 tbsp. molasses

1 (46 oz.) can pineapple rings
(reserve juice)

½ cup brown mustard

3 tbsp. dry hot mustard

1 tsp. cloves, ground

3 tbsp. frozen orange juice,
concentrate

1 (6-8 lb.) spiral ham

Pineapple-
Glazed Ham

Directions

1. Preheat the oven to 375° F.

2. In a bowl, mix together the brown sugar, molasses, juice from the pineapple, both mustards, cloves, and orange juice.

3. Put the ham into the Copper Chef. Attach the pineapple rings around the ham with toothpicks.

4. Pour the glaze over the ham. Put the Copper Chef in the oven for 1 hour.

5. Serve

Teriyaki Pork Tenderloins

Ingredients

1 tbsp. fresh ginger, minced (or 1 tsp. dried ginger)

4 scallions, chopped

2 cloves garlic, peeled and minced

2 tbsp. brown sugar

¼ cup soy sauce

1 cup white wine

2 tbsp. rice vinegar

2 pork tenderloins, trimmed (about 1 lb.)

3 tbsp. olive oil

Directions

1. Mix the ginger, scallions, garlic, brown sugar, soy sauce, white wine, and rice vinegar together. Reserve half of the mixture.

2. In the refrigerator, marinate pork tenderloin in half of the sauce for at least 1 hour.

3. Preheat the oven to 375° F.

4. Place the Copper Chef on medium-high heat. When the pan is hot, add the olive oil. Brown the pork on both sides.

5. Place the Copper Chef in the oven. Cook for about 20 minutes until the internal temperature is 155° F.

6. Remove from the oven. Pour the remaining sauce over the pork. Let rest for 15 minutes before serving.

Eric's Tip: This dish is delicious served over rice with fresh steamed broccoli.

Ingredients

3 pie crusts

2 cups onion, chopped

3 cups Swiss cheese, chopped

2 cups bacon, chopped

10 eggs

8 cups half and half

1 tbsp. cayenne pepper

1 tbsp. paprika

½ tbsp. sea salt

½ tbsp. ground black pepper

1 tsp. nutmeg

Quiche Lorraine

Directions

1. Preheat the oven to 375° F.

2. Drape the 3 pie crusts on the bottom and sides of the Copper Chef pan.

3. Add the onions, bacon, and Swiss cheese to the pan.

4. In a bowl, mix the eggs, half and half, spices, sea salt, and black pepper.

5. Pour the egg mixture into the Copper Chef. Stir gently.

6. Place the Copper Chef into the oven. Cook for 1-1½ hours until firm.

7. Let cool for about 20 minutes before serving.

Eric's Tip: For a richer quiche, use heavy cream instead of half and half.

Ingredients

6 cups diced potatoes, blanched (or frozen hash browns)

water, to boil potatoes

3 tbsp. olive oil

1 medium onion, chopped

24 eggs, beaten

1 tbsp. basil

1 tbsp. onion powder

1 tbsp. paprika

1 lb. ham steak, diced

1 tsp. sea salt

1 tbsp. ground black pepper

1 cup heavy cream

1 lb. cheddar cheese, shredded, split into 2 batches

1 cup parsley, chopped, ¼ cup reserved for garnish

Giant Frittata

Directions

1. Preheat the oven to 350° F.

2. Add the potatoes to the Copper Chef. Cover with water. Bring the potatoes to a boil and simmer for 5 minutes. Drain. Set potatoes aside in a separate bowl. (Skip this step if using frozen potatoes.)

3. Heat the Copper Chef on medium-high heat. When the pan is hot, add the olive oil. Sauté the onions, basil, onion powder, paprika, and parsley for about 5 minutes. Season with sea salt and black pepper.

4. Add the ham. Cook for 2 minutes.

5. Add the potatoes. Stir well. Add the eggs, heavy cream, and half of the cheddar cheese. Stir until all ingredients are incorporated.

6. Place in the oven for 2 hours or until done.

7. Top with remaining cheddar cheese. Cover with lid to let the cheese melt.

8. Garnish with parsley before serving.

Eric's Tip: I love heating up the leftovers the next morning wrapped in a tortilla with fresh salsa.

Bleu Cheese Stuffed Mushrooms

Ingredients

30 medium mushrooms, stems and caps separated; stems chopped

4 tbsp. butter

1 shallot, peeled and minced

2 cloves garlic, peeled and minced

1 onion, peeled and minced

½ red pepper, seeded and diced small

1 sprig thyme, leaves removed and chopped

1½ cups breadcrumbs

½ cup bleu cheese, crumbled

Directions

1. Preheat the oven to 400° F.

2. Chop the mushrooms stems in a food processor.

3. Place the Copper Chef on medium-high heat. Add the butter and sweat the shallot, garlic, onion, and red pepper with the chopped mushroom stems.

4. Add the thyme, breadcrumbs, and bleu cheese. Remove from heat and mix well.

5. Stuff the mushroom caps with the filling. Put into a cleaned Copper Chef and place into the oven.

6. Cook for 20-25 minutes.

7. Serve.

Ingredients

1 lb. red potatoes, ¼-inch sliced

1 lb. salmon fillet

1 lb. sea scallops

juice of 1 fresh lime

2 tbsp. olive oil

½ cup onion, sliced

¾ cup heavy cream

⅓ cup fresh cilantro, chopped

½ cup green bell pepper, sliced

1 clove garlic, crushed

Lime Cilantro Seafood Bake

Directions

1. Preheat the oven to 350° F.

2. In the Copper Chef, combine olive oil, sliced potatoes, onions, green bell peppers, and garlic. Toss until combined. Place in the oven for 15 minutes until tender.

3. Cut salmon and scallops into ¾-inch dice. In a large bowl, toss the seafood in lime juice.

4. Take the potatoes out of the oven. Add the heavy cream and cilantro. Stir.

5. Using a slotted spoon, top the potatoes with salmon and scallops. Stir to incorporate.

6. Finish cooking in the oven for another 15-20 minutes.

7. Let cool before serving.

Eric's Tip: Sometimes I crack a few eggs on top in the last 10 minutes of cooking for a fantastic brunch dish.

Ingredients

3 large eggplants, sliced

1 tbsp. salt

2 cups flour

6 eggs

¼ cup milk

3 cups seasoned breadcrumbs

1 tsp. oregano, dried

½ cup olive oil, plus more as needed

4 cups tomato sauce

2 lb. mozzarella, sliced

¼ cup Parmesan, grated

Eggplant Parmesan

Directions

1. Slice the eggplants. Lightly salt each slice and place in a colander to allow the natural water to drain out for about 30-60 minutes.

2. Pour the flour into a flat pan or a large bowl. In a second bowl, mix the eggs and the milk. Put the breadcrumbs in a flat pan. Set in a row for breading.

3. Place the Copper Chef on medium-high heat. Add ½ cup of olive oil to start.

4. One slice at a time, dip the eggplant into the flour, then the egg, and finally into the breadcrumbs. Carefully brown the eggplant on both sides in the Copper Chef. You will need to add olive oil at different times throughout the cooking process as the eggplant absorbs oil like a sponge.

5. Put the eggplant on paper towels to absorb any excess oil.

6. Wipe out the Copper Chef. Preheat the oven to 375° F.

7. Pour 1 cup of tomato sauce on the bottom of the Copper Chef. Layer the cooked eggplant with mozzarella cheese and tomato sauce. Save enough tomato sauce and mozzarella cheese for the top.

8. Place into the oven with the lid on for 40 minutes. Remove the lid and cook 10 additional minutes.

9. Remove from the oven and let cool for 10-15 minutes.

10. Top with grated Parmesan cheese before serving.

Eric's Tip: Eggplant is naturally full of water. The reason you drain the water out of the eggplant using salt in step 1 is to achieve a less watery, firmer fried eggplant. Don't worry, most of the salt falls out with the water.

Ingredients

4 lb. red potatoes, sliced thin

2 onions, chopped

4 tbsp. butter

1 qt. heavy cream

¾ lb. Swiss cheese, diced

1 cup grated Parmesan cheese

1 sprig rosemary, chopped

½ tsp. salt

½ tsp. ground black pepper

Au Gratin Potatoes

Directions

1. Preheat the oven to 350° F.

2. Place the Copper Chef on low heat. Melt the butter. Sweat the onions for about 5 minutes. Remove half and set aside.

3. Remove from the heat and layer the potatoes, onions, Swiss and Parmesan cheeses. Save one layer of both cheeses for the top.

4. Pour the cream over the potatoes. Add rosemary, salt, and black pepper. Top with both cheeses and place in the oven.

5. Cook at 350° F for 2 – 2.5 hours or until nicely browned on top.

Eric's Tip: Transform this traditional recipe into Loaded Baked Potato Gratin: use cheddar instead of Swiss, then top with crispy bacon crumbles and chives!

SERVES 10-12

Ingredients

4 cups spaghetti sauce (from a jar or homemade)

1 lb. spaghetti, cooked

2 cups ricotta cheese

5 eggs

2 cups mozzarella, shredded

1 cup Parmesan cheese, grated

2 lb. ground beef, browned and drained

½ cup fresh parsley, chopped

Spaghetti Pie

Directions

1. Preheat the oven to 350° F.

2. Pour 1 cup spaghetti sauce into the Copper Chef. Add ¼ lb. of the spaghetti.

3. In a bowl, mix together eggs, cheeses, and parsley.

4. Pour the ricotta mix into the Copper Chef. Spread evenly.

5. Place another layer of the spaghetti on top.

6. Mix the meat with 1 cup spaghetti sauce. Pour the meat on top of the spaghetti layer.

7. Place the rest of the spaghetti on top. Pour the rest of the sauce over the spaghetti. Add the remainder of the cheeses. Cook in the oven for about 45 minutes.

8. Let rest for 20-30 minutes before serving.

Eric's Tip: Turn this recipe into a delicious Alfredo pie by using Parmesan cream sauce, one cup of frozen peas, and one cup of diced ham.

Sweet Potatoes with Marshmallows

Ingredients

1 stick butter, melted

4 lb. sweet potatoes, peeled and sliced thin

2/3 cup maple syrup

¼ cup chicken stock

¼ tsp nutmeg

½ tsp. cinnamon

½ tsp. sea salt

1 bag miniature marshmallows

Directions

1. Preheat the oven to 350° F.

2. Place half of the melted butter into the Copper Chef.

3. In a bowl, mix the maple syrup, chicken stock, spices, and sea salt together.

4. Layer the sweet potatoes in the Copper Chef. Pour the maple syrup mixture in-between the layers. Top with remaining butter.

5. Cover the Copper Chef. Place into the oven for 1 to 1½ hours.

6. After 1 hour, test with a knife to see if the potatoes are tender.

7. Remove the lid. Add the marshmallows to the top. Cook for another 20 minutes until lightly toasted.

Ingredients

1 lb. ziti, cooked

2 cups ricotta cheese

1½ cups mozzarella, shredded

¾ cup Parmesan cheese, grated

8 cooked meatballs, crushed

4 eggs

4 cups tomato sauce

Baked Ziti

Directions

1. Preheat the oven to 350° F.

2. In a large bowl, combine the ziti pasta, ricotta, 1 cup mozzarella, ½ cup Parmesan cheese, crushed meatballs, and eggs. Add half of the tomato sauce. Mix.

3. Pour 1 cup tomato sauce on the bottom of the Copper Chef. Pour the pasta mixture into the pan and smooth it out.

4. Pour the rest of the tomato sauce on top. Spread evenly. Sprinkle the rest of the mozzarella and grated Parmesan cheese on top.

5. Cover with the lid. Place in the oven for 45 minutes to 1 hour.

6. Let cool before serving.

Eric's Tip: This is a great meal to make a day ahead of time because you can refrigerate it before you bake it.

Ingredients

1 lb. egg noodles

water, to boil egg noodles

½ stick butter

6 eggs

2 cups cottage cheese

2 cups sour cream

¾ cup sugar

1 tsp. vanilla extract

½ cup milk

Topping:

½ cup brown sugar

½ cup sugar

1 tbsp. cinnamon

Noodle Kugel

Directions

1. Fill the Copper Chef ¾ of the way with water. Bring to a boil. Cook egg noodles until tender. Strain.

2. Preheat the oven to 350° F.

3. Toss the egg noodles with butter.

4. In a bowl, mix the eggs, cottage cheese, sour cream, sugar, vanilla extract, and milk.

5. Toss the egg noodles with the egg mixture. Pour into the Copper Chef.

6. In a bowl, mix the topping ingredients. Sprinkle on top.

7. Cover. Place in the oven for 45-60 minutes.

8. Let cool for 30 minutes before serving.

Eric's Tip: I like this dish with raisins on the top. Put them on after you take it out of the oven.

Vegetable Lasagna

Ingredients

2 tbsp. olive oil

1 onion, peeled and sliced

1½ cups mushrooms

3 cups ricotta

3 eggs

¼ cup fresh basil, chopped

½ cup fresh parsley, chopped

½ tsp. dry oregano

2 cups spinach, cooked

2 cups mozzarella shredded

1 cup Parmesan cheese, grated

3 cups tomato sauce

3 zucchini, sliced lengthwise thin

3 yellow squash, sliced lengthwise, thin

6 roasted red peppers

Directions

1. Preheat the oven to 350° F.

2. Place the Copper Chef on medium-high heat. When the pan is hot, add the olive oil. Sauté the onions and mushrooms until tender. Place in a dish and set aside.

3. In a bowl, mix together the ricotta, eggs, basil, parsley, oregano, 1½ cups mozzarella, spinach, and ½ cup of grated Parmesan cheese. Set aside.

4. In the Copper Chef, pour 1 cup of tomato sauce and lay ½ of the zucchini slices across the bottom.

5. Pour in the mushrooms and onions. Spread evenly. Place a layer of yellow squash on top. Spread 1/3 of the ricotta cheese mix on top.

6. Layer roasted red peppers and 1 cup tomato sauce. Add another layer of the ricotta mixture. Top with second half of zucchini slices.

7. Add a final layer of ricotta mixture. Top with yellow squash and tomato sauce. Sprinkle the rest of the mozzarella and grated Parmesan cheese on top.

7. Place the Copper Chef in the oven, covered. After 1 hour, remove the lid and cook for 20 more minutes.

Eric's Tip: Make a heartier meal by adding a mix of ground pork, veal, and beef to your sauce.

Decadent
Baked Desserts

Blueberry Breakfast Cake with Crumb Topping

Coffee Cake

Black Forest Cake

Coconut Cake

Peanut Butter Brownies

Cornbread

Baklava

Pumpkin Cake

Banana Nut Bread

Sticky Buns

Cheesecake Brownies

Usually we think of our pots and pans as tools for cooking main meals, but with the Copper Chef's unique design, you can bake cakes, brownies, rice puddings, and many other desserts in it, also! Desserts are known for their difficult clean-up due to the sugar content and subsequent carmelization, but with the advanced ceramic nonstick in Copper Chef, clean-up couldn't be easier. We even designed the corners to be slightly rounded, which means cakes and other desserts literally fall right out once cooled.

Blueberry Breakfast Cake with Crumb Topping

SERVES 9

Ingredients

½ lb. butter, soft

2 cups sugar

2 eggs

3 tsp. vanilla extract

1 cup milk

4 cups flour

1 tsp. cinnamon

1 tbsp. baking powder

1 tsp. salt

2 cups fresh blueberries

Crumb Topping:

⅔ cup flour

½ cup cold butter

1 cup light brown sugar

1 tsp. cinnamon

Directions

1. Preheat the oven to 350° F.

2. In an electric mixer, cream the butter with the sugar. Add one egg at a time until incorporated well. Add the milk and vanilla. Mix well.

3. In a separate bowl, mix the flour, baking powder, cinnamon, and salt. Slowly incorporate the flour mixture into the butter mixture. Mix just enough until well blended. Fold in fresh blueberries.

4. Pour batter into the Copper Chef and spread evenly.

5. For the crumb topping: in a bowl, add the flour and cold butter. Mix until the butter looks like the size of peas. Mix in the rest of the ingredients and top the blueberry cake batter.

6. Place the Copper Chef pan in the oven until the cake is done, about 1½ hours. To test, place a toothpick in the center. If the toothpick comes out clean, it is done.

Eric's Tip: The beauty of this recipe is that you can use any fruit that's fresh and in season. For larger fruit like peaches, cut into ½-inch dice.

Ingredients

1 stick butter

1 cup sugar

2 eggs

¾ cup milk

2 tsp. vanilla extract

1 tsp. cinnamon

3 cups flour

2 tsp. baking powder

½ tsp. salt

Topping:

4 tbsp. butter

1 cup dark brown sugar

2 cup flour

2 tsp. cinnamon

Coffee Cake

Directions

1. Preheat the oven to 350° F.

2. In an electric mixer, cream the butter with the sugar. Add one egg at a time until well incorporated. Add the milk, vanilla extract, and cinnamon. Mix well.

3. Mix the flour, baking powder and salt. Slowly add the flour mixture to the butter mixture until all incorporated.

4. Pour into the Copper Chef and spread evenly.

5. For the topping: mix flour and butter until the butter looks like the size of peas. Mix the rest of the ingredients and top the coffee cake batter.

6. Place in the oven until done, about 1½ hours. One way to test doneness is to place a toothpick in the center; if the toothpick comes out clean, it is done.

Eric's Tip: I like to dust this cake with powdered sugar at the end. It's also great toasted with butter.

Ingredients

4 eggs

1¼ cups milk

⅔ cup vegetable oil

2 tsp. vanilla extract

2½ cups sugar

3 cups flour

1 cup cocoa powder

2 tsp. baking powder

1 tsp. baking soda

1 tsp. salt

Filling:

1 bag frozen cherries, dark and sweet

2 tbsp. sugar

Whipped cream topping:

1 qt. heavy cream

¼ cup sugar

2 tsp. vanilla extract

Black Forest Cake

Directions

1. Preheat the oven to 350° F.

2. Mix together the wet ingredients in a large bowl.

3. Mix together all the dry ingredients. Incorporate dry ingredients into the wet ingredients. Pour cake batter into the Copper Chef and put into the oven.

4. Bake about 1 hour or until an inserted toothpick comes out clean. Let cool 20 minutes before removing from the Copper Chef. Put on a baking rack to cool.

5. Make the filling in the cleaned Copper Chef: add all the filling ingredients to the pan. Cover and bring to a boil until slightly thickened. Remove from heat and cool in the refrigerator for 30 minutes.

6. For whipped cream topping: add the heavy cream, sugar, and vanilla extract to an electric mixer bowl. Whip until stiff.

7. Assemble the cake: cut the cake in half so you have a top and a bottom.

8. Pour the cherry mixture on top of the bottom layer of cake. Cover with the remaining layer of cake.

9. Frost the cake, then chill before serving.

Coconut Cake

Ingredients

2 classic white cake mixes (do not follow box directions)

1 tsp. coconut extract

1 cup coconut milk

1 cup water

5 eggs

3 cups shredded coconut (for topping)

Coconut Frosting:

1 ½ cups butter

9 cups confectioners sugar

½ cup milk

1 tbsp. coconut extract

Directions

1. Preheat the oven to 350° F.

2. Using an electric mixer, place the cake mixes into a bowl. Add all of the ingredients. Mix well.

3. Pour batter into the Copper Chef. Bake until done, about 70 minutes. You can tell when the cake is done by placing a toothpick into the middle. When it comes out clean, it's done.

4. When the cake is done, remove from the oven and set aside for 45 minutes or until cool. Once the cake is cooled, carefully remove from the pan and place on a cooling rack.

5. Make the frosting: place the butter in the clean mixer bowl. Cream until smooth. Add the confectioners sugar and coconut extract. Alternate with the milk until creamy.

6. Once the cake is completely cooled, flip it over and cut horizontally into 2 pieces. Remove the top layer and set aside.

7. Frost the center of the cake about ½ inch thick. Place the top layer of the cake back on. Frost the sides and then the top. Once the cake is frosted, apply the shredded coconut to the top and sides.

Eric's Tip: Using chocolate cake mix and a drizzle of caramel sauce on top can take this recipe to the next level!

Ingredients

1 box brownie mix

1½ cups peanut butter

2 cups semi-sweet chocolate chips

Peanut Butter Brownies

Directions

1. Preheat the oven to 350° F (or whatever temperature it says to use on the box).

2. Make the brownies following the directions on the box. Pour into the Copper Chef and place into the oven.

3. When done, set aside to cool. Carefully remove the brownies from the Copper Chef and set aside.

4. Spread the peanut butter evenly on top of the brownies. Place the brownies in the freezer for 1 hour.

5. Melt the chocolate chips in the Copper Chef. Remove the brownies from the freezer and set on a steamer tray. Place on top of a wax paper sheet to catch the excess chocolate.

6. Pour the melted chocolate over the peanut butter and spread with a cake spatula so you have a ¼-inch thick top. Place in the fridge to set.

7. With a hot knife, cut the brownies into 16 servings.

Eric's Tip: Get creative! I love to add my favorite toppings to the batter: coconut flakes, chocolate candies, walnuts... you can't go wrong!

Ingredients

1 cup butter, melted

1¼ cups sugar

4 eggs

1¾ cup milk

1 tsp. baking soda

2 cups cornmeal

2 cups flour

1 tsp. sea salt

2 jalapeños, seeded and diced

Cornbread

Directions

1. Preheat the oven to 375° F.

2. Place the wet ingredients, except jalapeños, in a bowl. Mix well.

3. In a separate bowl, mix the dry ingredients.

4. Add the dry ingredients to the wet ingredients. Add the jalapeños and mix until incorporated.

5. Pour the cornbread batter into the Copper Chef. Place the pan into the oven and cook for about 45-60 minutes. Check center with a toothpick for doneness.

6. When toothpick comes out clean, cornbread is done.

7. Serve.

Eric's Tip: I love to make this cornbread cheesy. Just add 1 cup shredded cheddar or Monterey Jack to the wet ingredients.

Ingredients

20 sheets phyllo dough

1½ lb. walnuts, chopped

1 cup butter, melted

16 cloves, whole

Syrup:

1 cup water

1 cup sugar

¼ tsp. salt

1 cinnamon stick

juice of ½ lemon

1 tbsp. Chartreuse

Baklava

Directions

1. For the syrup: place the water, sugar, salt, cinnamon stick, lemon juice, and Chartreuse into the Copper Chef. Stir and bring to a boil until mixture thickens into a syrup. Remove the Copper Chef pan from the heat and transfer the syrup to a microwave-safe bowl. Clean the Copper Chef pan.

2. Unwrap and unroll the phyllo dough. Place the Copper Chef on top of the dough. Cut the dough to fit the base of the pan. You should be able to cut 10 sheets of dough at a time with a sharp knife. Cover the phyllo dough with a damp towel to keep it from drying out.

3. Preheat the oven to 375° F.

4. In a cleaned Copper Chef, layer 1 sheet of phyllo dough at a time. Lightly brush each sheet with the melted butter. Repeat this step until you have 10 sheets layered on top of each other.

5. Evenly spread 1 lb. of the chopped walnuts on the phyllo dough sheets.

6. Layer 10 more sheets of phyllo dough on top of the chopped walnuts. Brush each sheet with melted butter as you did with the first batch in step 4.

7. Cut the baklava into 16 triangles. Stick a clove in the center of each triangle.

8. Place the Copper Chef into the oven and bake for 45 minutes. Rotate the pan every 15 minutes.

9. Remove the cinnamon stick from the syrup. Reheat in the microwave for a few seconds until syrup is pourable, then pour over the baklava.

10. Spread the rest of the chopped walnuts on top.

11. Let baklava cool before serving.

Ingredients

3 cups sugar

1½ cups vegetable oil

1 tsp. vanilla

2 tsp. cinnamon

½ tsp. nutmeg

¼ tsp. cloves

½ tsp. salt

2½ cups pumpkin, cooked

5 eggs

3 cups flour

1 tbsp. baking powder

2 tsp. baking soda

Pumpkin Cake

Directions

1. Preheat the oven to 375° F.

2. In a large bowl, mix all of the wet ingredients together.

3. Fold in all of the dry ingredients until just mixed. Do not overmix.

4. Pour the batter into the Copper Chef and put into the oven.

5. Bake for 1 hour or until toothpick inserted into the center comes out clean.

Eric's Tip: I like to use this cake leftover for "crispy French toast" the next morning. Just dip a slice of pumpkin cake into any French toast batter and cook in the Copper Chef until lightly golden-brown on each side. Serve with butter and syrup.

Ingredients

6 bananas, overripe and smashed

¾ cup butter

3 eggs

½ cup milk

1 tsp. vanilla extract

2 cups sugar

3½ cups flour

1 tsp. salt

1 tsp. baking soda

¾ cup walnuts

Banana Nut Bread

Directions

1. Preheat the oven to 350° F.

2. In a large bowl, mix together the wet ingredients with the bananas. Add the dry ingredients and fold in the walnuts until just blended.

3. Pour the batter into Copper Chef. Place the Copper Chef in the oven. Cook until an inserted toothpick comes out clean (about 1½ hours).

4. Let banana nut bread cool before removing from the pan. Serve.

Eric's Tip: Make this recipe nut-free by substituting dried cranberries or coconut flakes for the walnuts.

Ingredients

½ tbsp. active dry yeast

½ cup milk, scalded

¼ cup water

¼ cup sugar

1 tsp. salt

2 eggs

3 tbsp. butter, melted

4½ cups flour

To brush dough:

1½ sticks butter, melted

Filling:

1 cup brown sugar

1 cup pecans, chopped

1 tsp. cinnamon

Sticky Buns

Directions

1. Place the yeast, milk, and water in an electric mixer. Add the rest of the ingredients except filling ingredients. The dough should form a ball.

2. Place dough in the Copper Chef. Cover and set in a warm place until dough doubles in size.

3. Make the filling: in a bowl, combine brown sugar, chopped pecans, and cinnamon.

4. Roll the dough out on a floured table about ¼" thick x 6" wide x 12 " long.

5. Cut 2" strips on the shortest side of the dough. Brush the strips with melted butter, then sprinkle with the brown sugar mixture. Roll the strips up and place into the Copper Chef. Repeat until all are done.

6. Cover Copper Chef with the lid. Place in the oven on warm until dough doubles in size.

7. Remove the Copper Chef lid and raise the oven temperature to 375° F.

8. Remove sticky buns from the oven and let cool before serving (about 20 minutes).

Eric's Tip: Calling all apple lovers! Reserve some of the brown sugar mixture to coat the bottom of the pan before baking. Top with fresh green apple slices. Place the buns on top of the apples & continue with oven directions.

Ingredients

1 cup butter, softened

1 cup sugar

3 eggs

2 tsp. vanilla extract

2 cups chocolate chips,
semi-sweet, melted

1 oz. espresso

1 tsp. salt

1½ cups flour

1 tsp. baking powder

Cheese Swirl:

1 (8 oz.) pack cream cheese

¼ cup sugar

½ tsp. vanilla extract

Cheesecake Brownies

Directions

1. Preheat the oven to 350º F.

2. In an electric mixer, blend the butter and sugar.

3. Add 1 egg at a time and mix well. Add the espresso, vanilla extract, and melted chocolate chips.

4. In another bowl, combine the salt, flour, and baking powder. Add to the butter mixture until blended.

5. Pour into the Copper Chef and smooth batter evenly.

6. In a clean, electric mixing bowl, blend the cream cheese, sugar, and vanilla extract together until creamy.

7. Drop spoonfuls of the cream cheese mixture throughout the brownie batter. Swirl with a knife.

8. Place the Copper Chef pan into the oven.

9. Cook until an inserted toothpick comes out clean, about 1 hour. Let brownies cool before serving.

Easy
Stir-Fried Favorites

Spicy Asian Beef Wraps

Steak and Soba Noodles

Pepper Steak

Pork Fried Rice

Asparagus, Bacon and Spinach

Shrimp and Asparagus

Mongolian Beef

Vegetable Fried Rice

Vegetable Lo Mein

A traditional stir-fry pan has high sides, a flat bottom, and a round shape. A traditional wok has a rounded concave bottom that has a special ring to allow it to sit flat on a flame or stovetop. Both of these require a very hot cooking temperature to work properly and get good results. Our ceramic nonstick can take heat up to 850° F, which allows us to cook any stir-fry or wok recipe right in the Copper Chef. Because of its high sides, similar to those found on a wok or stir-fry pan, and its slightly rounded corners, you can toss your stir-fry foods with ease. This is a fun technique for cooking quickly, allowing your food to stay bright and fresh.

Spicy Asian Beef Wraps

SERVES 2-4

Ingredients

1 tbsp. olive oil

1 lb. ground beef

1½ tbsp. soy sauce

2 tbsp. hoisin sauce

½ cup water chestnuts, chopped

1 cup mushrooms, chopped

1 clove garlic, chopped

⅓ cup scallion, chopped

¼ cup cilantro, chopped

1 tsp. toasted sesame oil

1 tsp. fresh ginger, minced

1 head Bibb lettuce

lime wedges, for garnish

julienned carrots, for garnish

bean sprouts, for garnish

Directions

1. Place the Copper Chef on medium-high heat. Add olive oil. Brown ground beef for 5-8 minutes. Drain excess grease and set aside in a bowl. Add mushrooms, water chestnuts, scallions, garlic, and ginger. Sauté for 5-8 minutes.

2. Add ground beef, soy sauce, sesame oil, and hoisin sauce. Cook for an additional 5 minutes until all the liquid has been absorbed.

3. Remove from heat. Toss in cilantro.

4. Serve in Bibb lettuce cups. Garnish with lime wedges, julienned carrots, and bean sprouts.

Eric's Tip: Be creative! Add more texture to your wraps with your favorite crunchy ingredients. I like using fried rice noodles or wontons.

Steak and Soba Noodles

Ingredients

1 flank steak

½ tbsp. sea salt

½ tbsp. ground black pepper

5 tbsp. olive oil

1 tsp. ginger, peeled and minced

3 cloves garlic, minced

4 scallions, chopped

1 onion, peeled and sliced

½ red pepper, seeded and sliced

3 baby bok choy, chopped

½ carrot, peeled and sliced

9 oz. soba noodles, cooked

2 tbsp. oyster sauce

¼ tsp. sesame oil

Directions

1. Season the flank steak with sea salt and black pepper. Cut into 2 or 3 pieces to fit into the bottom of the pan.

2. Place the Copper Chef on high heat. When the pan is hot, add 2 tbsp. olive oil. Sear the steak until desired temperature or about 130° F. Remove steak and set aside to rest.

3. Add the rest of the olive oil. Sauté the ginger, garlic, scallions, and vegetables on medium-high heat until tender. Lower the heat to medium. Add the noodles. Toss with the oyster sauce and sesame oil.

4. Slice the flank steak thin. Serve with soba noodles.

Eric's Tip: Cook the flank steak until it is a bit more rare than you want it to be at the end because it will continue to cook after it's set aside. If it suits your taste, this recipe really benefits from a medium-rare result at the end of the process.

Ingredients

1 tbsp. soy sauce

1 tsp. honey

½ tsp. onion powder

½ tsp garlic powder

2 tbsp. olive oil

½ tsp. ground black pepper

½ tsp. red pepper flakes

¾ lb. beef roast, eye of round, sliced into ¼" strips

½ yellow pepper, seeded and cut into strips

½ red pepper, seeded and cut into strips

1 onion, peeled and sliced

Pepper Steak

Directions

1. In a bowl, mix soy sauce, honey, red pepper flakes, onion powder, black pepper, garlic powder, and 1 tbsp. olive oil. Add the beef and coat evenly.

2. Place the Copper Chef on high heat. When preheated, add 1 tbsp. olive oil.

3. Add the onions & peppers to the pan. Cook for 4 minutes until tender. Remove and set aside.

4. Drain the meat and add to the Copper Chef pan. Cook until browned (about 4 minutes).

5. Add the onions and peppers back to the pan. Mix.

6. Serve steak over rice.

Eric's Tip: I love this steak leftover: wrap in a burrito with rice or top a nice, chilled salad of crispy greens.

Ingredients

2 (4 oz.) pork loins, cut into small cubes

5 tbsp. olive oil

¾ cup napa cabbage, chopped

1 carrot, peeled and diced small

1 onion, peeled and diced small

2 cloves garlic, peeled and minced

4 scallions, chopped

1 tsp. ginger fresh, peeled and minced

6 cups cooked white rice

2 eggs

1 cup peas

1 tbsp. soy sauce

½ tsp. ground black pepper

Pork Fried Rice

Directions

1. Place the Copper Chef on high heat. When the pan is hot, add 2 tbsp. olive oil. Brown the pork loin. Remove and set aside.

2. Sauté the napa cabbage, carrots, and onions in the Copper Chef. Remove and set aside.

3. Combine garlic, scallions, and ginger with the rest of the olive oil. Cook for 3 or 4 minutes, careful not to burn the garlic.

4. Reduce the heat to medium. Add the eggs and rice. Stir. Cook until the eggs are set up. Add the napa cabbage mix, peas, pork, and soy sauce. Stir. Cook for 3 more minutes. Season with black pepper before serving.

Eric's Tip: It's easy to use chicken or shrimp instead of pork if you prefer!

Asparagus, Bacon and Spinach

Ingredients

2 tbsp. olive oil

½ lb. bacon, diced

1 lb. asparagus, cut into thirds

1 tsp. ginger, fresh, peeled and minced

2 cloves garlic, peeled and minced

4 cups baby spinach, fresh

½ tsp. sea salt

1 tbsp. lemon zest

Directions

1. Place the Copper Chef on medium heat. Cook the bacon until crispy. Remove the bacon and drain the oil.

2. Add the olive oil to the Copper Chef. Sear the asparagus until tender. Remove and set aside.

3. Add the ginger and garlic to the pan. Cook for 2 or 3 minutes, careful not to burn the garlic.

4. Add the spinach. Stir ingredients, then reduce the heat and cover with the lid. Cook until the spinach is wilted.

5. Remove the lid. Add everything back into the Copper Chef.

6. Season with sea salt and lemon zest. Toss and serve.

Eric's Tip: If you like a little heat, this is great with about ¼-½ tsp. red pepper flakes added at the last step.

Shrimp and Asparagus

Ingredients

1 lb. large shrimp, peeled and deveined

1 lb. asparagus, trimmed & cut into bite-sized pieces

¼ cup. olive oil

1 clove garlic, peeled and minced

1 tsp. ginger, peeled and minced

1 tbsp. soy sauce

2 tbsp. oyster sauce

2 tbsp. rice wine

½ tsp. black pepper

Directions

1. Place the Copper Chef on high heat. When the pan is hot, add half the olive oil. Sear the shrimp. Remove and set aside.

2. Add the rest of the olive oil. Sauté the asparagus, tossing steadily until tender, but firm.

3. Add the garlic, ginger, and shrimp. Sauté for 3 or 4 minutes, careful not to burn the garlic.

4. Add the rest of the ingredients. Stir.

5. Remove from heat and serve immediately.

Ingredients

Marinade:

3 tbsp. soy sauce

2 tbsp. brown sugar

1 tsp. dried ginger

1 tbsp. sesame oil

1 tbsp. cornstarch

4 scallions, chopped

Sauce:

1 tbsp. ginger, peeled and minced

3 cloves garlic, peeled and minced

½ cup brown sugar

⅓ cup soy sauce

⅓ cup water

3 tbsp. olive oil

1 flank steak, sliced thin

Mongolian Beef

Directions

1. In a bowl, mix all of the marinade ingredients together. Pour over the steak and stir. Allow steak to marinate for at least an hour.

2. Place the Copper Chef on medium-high heat. Add all of the sauce ingredients except olive oil. Boil for 4 minutes. Pour sauce into a container and set aside.

3. Place the cleaned Copper Chef on high heat. When the pan is hot, add the olive oil. Add in the steak and brown. When almost done, toss with the sauce.

4. Serve steak and sauce over rice.

Eric's Tip: Cooking the flank steak really fast on high heat sears in the juices and the flavors. This is the same technique used on a hot Mongolian grill.

Vegetable Fried Rice

Ingredients

3 tbsp. olive oil

8 shiitake mushrooms, sliced

3 baby bok choy, chopped

1 carrot, peeled and diced small

1 small onion, peeled and diced small

½ red pepper, seeded and diced small

1 small can water chestnuts, chopped

2 cloves garlic, peeled and minced

4 scallions, chopped

6 cups cooked white rice

2 eggs

1 cup peas, cooked

1 tbsp. soy sauce

1 tsp. ginger, fresh, peeled and minced

½ tsp ground black pepper

Directions

1. Place the Copper Chef on high heat. When the pan is hot, add the olive oil and shiitake mushrooms. Sauté for about 2 minutes.

2. Add the bok choy, carrot, onion, red pepper, water chestnuts, garlic, scallions, and ginger. Cook for 3 or 4 minutes or until the bok choy is tender.

3. Add the eggs and rice. Cook, stirring constantly until the eggs are set up.

4. Add the peas, soy sauce, and black pepper. Stir until incorporated. Lower heat to medium-low.

5. Cover with the lid. Cook for about 2 more minutes before serving.

Eric's Tip: Fried rice is extra yummy topped with toasted sesame seeds.

Vegetable Lo Mein

Ingredients

6 shiitake mushrooms, stems removed & sliced

3 tbsp. olive oil

10 snow peas

1 small onion, peeled and diced small

½ red pepper, seeded and diced small

2 cloves garlic, peeled and minced

4 scallions, chopped

1 tsp. ginger, fresh, peeled and minced

6 cups cooked lo mein noodles

1 cup spinach

1 tbsp. sweet soy sauce

1 tsp. sriracha sauce

½ tsp. sesame oil

Directions

1. Place the Copper Chef on high heat. When the pan is hot, add half of the olive oil. Sear the shiitake mushrooms. Remove and set aside.

2. Add the rest of the olive oil. Stir-fry the snow peas, onion, and red pepper until tender.

3. Add the garlic, scallions, ginger, and shiitake mushrooms to the pan. Sauté for 3 or 4 minutes, careful not to burn the garlic.

4. Add the lo mein, spinach, sweet soy sauce, sriracha, and sesame oil. Stir.

5. Remove from heat and serve.

Eric's Tip: Trying to add protein? In this recipe, I suggest searing shrimp along with the shiitake mushrooms.

Home-Cooked
Soups & Chilies

Cream of Mushroom

White Bean

Split Pea

Roasted Cauliflower Soup
with Brown Butter

Thai Coconut Chicken Soup

New England Clam Chowder

Shrimp Gumbo

Shrimp Bisque

Eric's Beef Chili

Seafood Bouillabaisse

Classic Beef Barley

Tortilla Soup

Pozole Guerrero

Eric's French Quarter Chili

Super Easy Turkey Chili

The reason people love their Copper Chef is because they only need one pan to steam, deep-fry, stir-fry, sauté, braise, roast, and bake their recipes. The large capacity lends itself to making family-sized soup and chili portions. Soups and chilies are infamous for staining pots due to their longer cooking times. I love cooking my soups and chilies in the Copper Chef because the ceramic nonstick makes this problem a non-issue. You can just wipe it out or simply put it in the dishwasher. It comes out clean every time!

Ingredients

½ lb. butter

1 large onion, peeled and minced

2 shallots, peeled and minced

3 stalks celery, diced small

6 cups mushrooms, chopped

1/3 cup flour

6 cups chicken stock

2 sprigs tarragon, chopped

1 bay leaf

1 tsp. salt

1 tsp. ground black pepper

1 cup heavy cream

Cream of Mushroom

Directions

1. Place the Copper Chef on medium-high heat. Melt the butter. Cover and sweat the onion, shallots, celery, and mushrooms until tender.

2. Sprinkle the flour on the vegetables. Stir. Cook for 4 minutes.

3. Whisk in the chicken stock until creamy. Add the tarragon and bay leaf.

4. Simmer for 30 minutes.

5. Season with salt and pepper. Stir in the heavy cream.

6. Remove the bay leaf and allow to cool slightly.

7. Place in a blender. Pulse carefully until chunky.

8. Serve.

Eric's Tip: For a heartier soup, I love adding bacon. Sauté as much or as little as you like along with the onion, shallots, celery, and mushrooms. Or, crumble and use as a garnish!

Ingredients

2 tbsp. olive oil

½ lb. bacon

1 large onion, peeled and diced

2 carrots, peeled and diced

2 stalks celery, diced

1 (16 oz.) bag navy beans

1 bay leaf

½ tbsp. salt

1 tsp. ground black pepper

1 tsp. granulated garlic

2 sprigs rosemary

8 cups chicken stock

White Bean

Directions

1. Place the Copper Chef on medium-high heat. When the pan is hot, add olive oil to brown bacon.

2. Add the vegetables. Sweat until tender.

3. Add the beans, chicken stock, herbs, and seasoning. Bring to a boil.

4. Reduce to a simmer. Cook until the beans are tender, about 1 hour.

Eric's Tip: This soup pairs perfectly with fresh bruschetta!

Ingredients

2 tbsp. olive oil

2 ham hocks, smoked

1 large onion, peeled and diced

2 carrots, peeled and diced

2 stalks celery, diced

1 (16 oz.) bag green split peas

1 bay leaf

½ tbsp. salt

1 tsp. ground black pepper

1 tsp. granulated onion

½ tsp. clove

8 cups chicken stock

Split Pea

Directions

1. Place the Copper Chef on medium-high heat. When the pan is hot, add olive oil. Sweat the vegetables while covered.

2. Add the ham hocks, split peas, chicken stock, herbs, and seasoning. Bring to a boil. Reduce to a simmer.

3. Cook until the soup is thick and creamy, about 90 minutes.

4. Remove the ham hocks. Set aside to let cool for 10 minutes.

5. Remove about 3 cups of soup. Process in a blender or food processor until very smooth. Pour back into the pan.

6. Take any remaining meat off of the ham hocks. Cut into bite size pieces before returning to the soup.

7. Adjust the seasoning with salt and black pepper before serving.

Eric's Tip: This soup is delicious topped with crunchy, garlic croutons.

Roasted Cauliflower Soup with Brown Butter

SERVES 4-6

Ingredients

1 large head of cauliflower (2-2½ pounds)

¾ cup water

1 tsp. thyme

salt and pepper

2 cloves garlic, peeled and minced

7 tbsp. butter

½ cup onion, peeled and diced

4 cups vegetable stock

1 cup cream

2 tsp. chives, chopped, for garnish

Directions

1. Preheat the oven to 350° F.

2. Break cauliflower into smaller florets. Place in Copper Chef with water, thyme, salt, and pepper. Cover with lid. Bake for 20-25 minutes until tender. Let cool, then remove and chop.

3. Melt 3 tbsp. butter in the pan. Sauté onions until caramelized.

4. Add cauliflower, vegetable stock, and cream. Stir and simmer for 8-10 minutes. Let cool, then purée.

5. In a clean Copper Chef, add remaining butter. Cook on medium heat for 5-8 minutes until the milk solids turn light brown with a nutty aroma.

6. After plating the soup, drizzle brown butter on top. Garnish with chopped chives before serving.

Eric's Tip: Feel free to substitute cauliflower for broccoli, parsnips, or acorn squash.

Thai Coconut Chicken Soup

Ingredients

3 tbsp. olive oil

1 tbsp. ginger, peeled and minced

2 cloves garlic, peeled and minced

6 scallions, chopped

1 onion, peeled and diced

1 carrot, peeled and diced small

1 red pepper, seeded and diced small

6 cups chicken stock

2 chicken breasts, trimmed

1 (13.5 oz.) can coconut milk

1 Thai pepper, chopped

8 basil leaves, chopped

2 tbsp. cilantro, chopped

Directions

1. Place the Copper Chef on medium-high heat. When the pan is hot, add the olive oil, ginger, garlic, and scallions. Sauté for 2 minutes, careful not to burn the garlic. Add the onion, carrot, and red pepper. Lower the heat to medium-low. Sweat, covered, for about 5 minutes.

2. Add the chicken stock, chicken breasts, and coconut milk. Stir and lower heat to simmer for 30 minutes.

3. Remove the chicken breasts and shred it. Return into the soup with the Thai pepper, basil, and cilantro.

4. Stir and Serve.

New England Clam Chowder

Ingredients

2 cups water

25 Littleneck clams, scrubbed

¼ cup butter

½ lb. bacon, diced

1 medium onion, peeled and diced

3 stalks celery, diced

½ red pepper, seeded and diced

¼ cup flour

6 cups clam broth

3 large white potatoes, diced

2 bay leaves

1 sprig thyme

¾ heavy cream

¼ cup dry sherry

2 (6.5 oz.) cans chopped clams, strained

½ tsp. sea salt

1 tsp. ground black pepper

½ cup chopped parsley

Directions

1. Pour 2 cups of water into the Copper Chef. Place on high heat. When the water is boiling, add the Littleneck clams. Steam until they open.

2. Remove the Littleneck clams and set aside. Strain remaining liquid and set aside.

3. In a clean Copper Chef on medium-high heat, add the bacon. Cook until almost crispy. Add butter, onions, celery, and red pepper. Cook until tender.

4. Stir in the flour. Cook for 4 minutes.

5. Whisk in the clam broth and reserved clam liquid from the cooked Littleneck clams.

6. Add the potatoes, bay leaves, and thyme. Simmer for 35 minutes.

7. Add the heavy cream, sherry, chopped clams, sea salt, and black pepper. Stir. Bring to a simmer for about 5 minutes. Do not boil.

8. Ladle the chowder into bowls. Drop a handful of the clams into each bowl.

9. Garnish with parsley and serve immediately.

Eric's Tip: When you serve the chowder, be sure to have a large bowl of oyster crackers and tobacco sauce at the ready.

Ingredients

3 tbsp. butter

1 onion, peeled and diced

2 cloves garlic, peeled and minced

1 shallot, peeled and minced

3 tbsp. flour

1 tbsp. tomato paste

2 stalks celery, diced

2 carrots, peeled and diced

8 okra, sliced

1 cup diced tomatoes

1 red pepper, seeded and diced

1 tsp. paprika

6 cups shrimp stock or chicken stock

½ tsp. cayenne pepper

1 bay leaf

1 sprig oregano, chopped

1 tsp. sea salt

½ tsp. ground black pepper

2 lb. medium shrimp, peeled and deveined

Shrimp Gumbo

Directions

1. Place the Copper Chef on medium-high heat. Add the butter and sweat the onions, garlic, and shallots.

2. Stir in the flour and tomato paste. Mix well.

3. Add the celery, carrots, okra, tomatoes, red peppers, and paprika. Stir. Cook for a few minutes covered on low.

4. Turn the heat to medium. Whisk in the shrimp stock until creamy.

5. Add the rest of the ingredients except the shrimp. Cook for 20 minutes, stirring occasionally.

6. Add the shrimp. Cook for another 15 minutes, stirring occasionally.

7. Serve.

Ingredients

3 tsp. butter + 1 tbsp. olive oil

1 lb. shrimp, peeled, deveined and quartered

3 carrots, chopped

3 stalks celery, chopped

3 shallots, chopped

¼ cup sundried tomatoes or tomato paste

½ tsp. paprika

1 pinch cayenne

½ cup brandy

2 cups heavy cream

4 cups seafood stock

½ cup instant potato flakes

2 tsp. fresh tarragon, chopped

salt and pepper

Shrimp Bisque

Directions

1. Place the Copper Chef on medium heat, Melt the butter in the oil. Sear the shrimp for 2 minutes or until pink and done. Remove and set shrimp aside.

2. Add carrots, celery, and shallots to the pan. Sweat for 6 minutes.

3. Add sundried tomatoes, paprika, and cayenne. Sweat uncovered for 2 more minutes.

4. Add the brandy. Stir and cook for another 2 minutes.

5. Cool for about 10 minutes. Add the shrimp and 1 cup seafood stock. Purée in a blender or food processor.

6. Pour the puréed mixture back into the pan. Add remaining seafood stock and the heavy cream. Stir well.

7. Add the potato flakes. Stir. Simmer on low for 20 minutes, stirring occasionally. Do not boil.

8. Finish with fresh tarragon. Adjust seasoning with salt and pepper before serving.

Ingredients

1 lb. 90/10 ground beef

2 lb. beef brisket, diced small

1 large onion, diced

2 tbsp. extra virgin olive oil

1 tbsp. extra virgin olive oil, to sauté peppers and onions

1 jalapeño, diced

2 large green bell peppers, diced

1 Anaheim pepper, diced

3 garlic cloves, smashed, then minced

1 (28 oz.) can chopped tomatoes

1 (15.5 oz.) can black beans

1 tbsp. tomato paste

½ cup white wine

1 cup beef stock

1 tbsp. balsamic vinegar

1/8 cup apple cider vinegar

¼ cup brown mustard

1 tbsp. cumin

1 tsp. coriander

2 tbsp. chili powder

½ tsp. cayenne pepper

¼ cup agave syrup (or brown sugar)

salt and pepper, to taste

Garnish:

½ cup parsley or cilantro, chopped

1 cup shredded cheddar cheese

1 cup sour cream

Eric's Beef Chili

Directions

1. Place the Copper Chef on high heat. When the pan is hot, add the extra virgin olive oil.

2. Brown the ground beef and beef brisket in batches. Drain the fat from the Copper Chef. Set ground beef and beef brisket aside.

3. Sauté the peppers and onions in olive oil until soft.

4. Add the ground beef and beef brisket to the onion and pepper mixture.

5. Add all of the remaining ingredients. Stir very well.

6. Cover and bring to a boil.

7. Reduce heat. Simmer for 30-40 minutes.

8. Serve with shredded cheddar cheese, sour cream, and chopped parsley or cilantro.

Eric's Tip: I like to stir in about 4 oz. dark chocolate at the very end to smooth out the flavors.

Ingredients

3 tbsp. olive oil

3 garlic cloves, peeled and minced

½ cup fennel, diced

1 onion, diced

1 shallot, peeled and minced

10 saffron threads

6 plum tomatoes, peeled and chopped

½ cup white wine

3 cups fish stock

1 bay leaf

3 sprigs fresh tarragon

1 lb. cod

¾ lb. medium to large shrimp, shelled and de-veined

20 mussels, scrubbed well, beards removed

20 clams

4 (4-5 oz.) lobster tails

Seafood Bouillabaisse

Directions

1. Preheat the Copper Chef on medium heat. Add olive oil. Sauté garlic, fennel, onion, saffron, and shallots for 3-4 minutes or until translucent.

2. Add the chopped plum tomatoes, white wine, fish stock, bay leaf, tarragon, cod, shrimp, mussels, clams, and lobster tails. Cover. Turn the heat up to medium-high.

3. Cook until the shellfish open, about 15 minutes.

4. Serve.

Eric's Tip: If saffron is unavailable, add 1 tbsp. paprika and 2 tsp. ground turmeric.

Ingredients

3 tbsp. olive oil

1 lb. stew beef, ½-inch diced

salt and pepper, for seasoning the meat

1 cup onion, peeled and diced

1 cup celery, diced

½ cup carrots, peeled and diced

1 cup parsnips, peeled and diced

1 cup cremini mushrooms, chopped

2 cloves garlic, peeled and minced

2 tbsp. tomato paste

1 tsp. rosemary, dry

¾ cup red wine

1 cup pearl barley, raw

4 cups beef broth

2 sprigs thyme, chopped

salt and pepper

Classic Beef Barley

Directions

1. Season the diced beef with salt and pepper.

2. Place the Copper Chef on high heat. When the pan is hot, add the olive oil. Sear the seasoned beef for 5 minutes. Remove and drain excess oil.

3. Add onion, celery, carrot, parsnips, cremini mushrooms, and garlic. Sweat vegetables for 6 minutes.

4. Stir in the tomato paste and dried rosemary. Deglaze with red wine.

5. Add beef back into the Copper Chef along with the pearl barley and beef broth. Stir well and cover.

6. Simmer for 30 minutes until beef and barley are tender.

7. Adjust seasoning with salt and pepper. Finish with fresh thyme before serving.

Eric's tip: Finish with 1 tbsp. of steak sauce for added zest.

Ingredients

3 tbsp. olive oil

1 onion, peeled and diced

1 red pepper, seeded and diced

3 cloves garlic, peeled and minced

6 plum tomatoes

1 (10 oz.) can of diced tomatoes with green chilies

1 cup cooked corn

6 cups chicken stock

¼ cup cilantro, chopped

3 cups tortilla chips, plus 1 cup for garnish

1 tsp. salt

1 tsp. cayenne pepper sauce

1 lime, cut into wedges

Tortilla Soup

Directions

1. Place the Copper Chef on medium-high heat. Add the olive oil when the pan is hot. Sweat the onion, red pepper, and garlic for 5 minutes.

2. Add plum tomatoes, diced tomatoes with green chilies, and the corn. Stir. Cook for 5 minutes.

3. Add the chicken stock. Cover and cook for 20 minutes on medium heat.

4. Add the cilantro, tortilla, salt, and cayenne pepper sauce.

5. Pour the soup into a blender or food processer. Pulse until puréed.

6. Garnish with tortillas. Squeeze some fresh lime juice into each bowl before serving.

Ingredients

1½ lb. pork shoulder, ½-inch cubed

1 cup onion, peeled and diced

½ cup poblano pepper, seeded and diced

4 cloves garlic, peeled and minced

1 (15 oz.) can hominy, rinsed and drained

6 cups chicken stock

1 (3 oz.) can salsa verde or tomatillos

2 tbsp. paprika

1 tbsp. cumin

½ tsp. dried oregano

salt and pepper

Garnish:

1 cup fresh cilantro, chopped

1 cup cabbage, shredded

2 avocados, diced

1 red onion, diced

Fresh lime wedges, one per bowl

2 cups tortilla chips

Pozole Guerrero

Directions

1. Place the Copper Chef on high heat. When the pan is hot, add pork shoulder, onion, poblano peppers, garlic, hominy, chicken stock, salsa verde, paprika, cumin, and oregano. Bring to a boil, then reduce heat and simmer for 60 minutes or until pork is tender.

2. Adjust seasoning with salt and pepper.

3. Ladle into bowls. Before serving, garnish with cilantro, shredded cabbage, diced avocados, onions, lime wedges, and chips.

Eric's tip: Substitute pork with shredded rotisserie chicken or shrimp. Just add during the last 10 minutes of cooking time.

Ingredients

2 tbsp. olive oil

1 lb. cooked Andouille sausage, diced

½ lb. cooked Spanish chorizo sausage, diced

1 lb. ground pork

1 tbsp. olive oil

1 cup onion, diced

1 jalapeño, diced

2 Anaheim peppers, diced

3 garlic cloves, peeled then minced

1 (28 oz.) can chopped tomatoes

1 tbsp. tomato paste

1 cup quality beer, preferably lager

2 cups beef stock

1/8 cup brown mustard

1 tbsp. cumin

1 tsp. coriander

1 (15.5 oz.) can black-eyed peas, drained

1 tbsp. Cajun blackening spice

¼-½ tsp. cayenne pepper (to your taste)

1 tbsp. honey

salt and pepper, to taste

Garnish:

½ cup parsley or cilantro, chopped

1 cup cheddar cheese, shredded

1 cup sour cream

Eric's French Quarter Chili

Directions

1. Place the Copper Chef on medium-high heat. Sauté Andouille sausage and Spanish chorizo for about 5 min to render the fat out. Drain fat and set aside.

2. On medium-high heat add 1 tbsp. of olive oil. Sauté the peppers and onions until tender.

3. Reduce heat to medium. Add the sausage and chorizo to the onion and pepper mixture. Stir.

4. Add all of the remaining ingredients (except the garnish). Stir well.

5. Place the lid on the Copper Chef. Cook for 10 min. on a high simmer. Uncover and simmer on medium-low heat for another 40 minutes.

6. Serve with shredded cheddar cheese, sour cream, and chopped parsley or cilantro.

Eric's Tip: I like to serve this chili over rice or egg noodles. Sometimes, in place of honey, I substitute balsamic glaze for a more pungent flavor.

Ingredients

4 tbsp. olive oil

1 lb. lean ground turkey

1 cup onion, chopped

1 cup green pepper, chopped

1 tbsp. jalapeño, chopped

2 tbsp. garlic, chopped

1 tbsp. cumin

1 tsp. dried oregano

1 tbsp. chili powder

1 (28.5 oz.) can crushed tomatoes

2 cups low sodium chicken stock

2 (14 oz.) cans great northern beans (or any bean of your choice), drained and rinsed

1 (6 oz.) can of salsa verde or tomatillos

salt and pepper

Garnish:

tortilla chips

cilantro, chopped

fresh lime juice

Super Easy Turkey Chili

Directions

1. Place the Copper Chef on medium heat. Add olive oil. Brown the ground turkey for about 5 minutes.

2. Add onion, green pepper, jalapeño, garlic, cumin, oregano, and chili powder. Sauté for 5 minutes.

3. Add crushed tomatoes, chicken stock, salsa verde, and beans of your choice. Cover. Simmer on low for 20 minutes. Take the lid off and simmer for another 10 minutes. Season with salt and pepper, to taste.

4. Garnish with tortilla strips, fresh chopped cilantro, and a squeeze of lime.

Eric's tip: Ground turkey can be easily substituted with a pre-cooked rotisserie chicken. Just add the chicken in at the end.

Steamed Selections

Cheese and Onion Pierogies

Greek Wonton Pot Stickers

Chicken and Scallion Pot Stickers

Pesto-Stuffed Flounder

New England Clam Bake

Halibut with Dijon and Tomato Drizzle

Herb-Steamed Shrimp

Steamed Salmon with Leeks and Asparagus

Whole Thai Steamed Snapper

Herb-Steamed Potatoes

Steamed Snow Crab Legs

Steaming is a great way to preserve the essential nutrients in your meals. Steaming cooks foods gently, which makes it a good technique for cooking delicate fish, for example. The problem is, most people don't have a steamer tray at the ready, and so this wonderful, healthy technique is often lost to most of us. Of course, you need to contain the steam inside the pan to create the ideal steaming environment. This is where our heavy and secure glass lid comes in handy.

Cheese and Onion Pierogies

Ingredients

1 (14 oz.) pack wonton wrappers (about 40 wrappers)

5 tbsp. butter

1 large onion, cut in half and sliced thin

¼ tsp. salt

¼ tsp. ground black pepper

½ cup sour cream

¼ cup chives

2 cups water

Filling:

2 lb. potatoes, cooked

1 cup ricotta cheese

1 onion, peeled, chopped, and sautéed

1 tsp. salt

½ tsp. ground black pepper

Directions

1. Reserve sour cream and chives. Make the filling: combine the rest of the ingredients in a large bowl.

2. Using a round cookie cutter, cut each wrapper into the largest circle possible.

3. Lay the circles onto a nonstick cookie sheet or floured surface.

4. Using your finger, rub the edges of the wontons with some water. Using a tablespoon, add enough filling into each wonton. Do not overstuff. Leave enough dough to press it closed, making a half moon. Use your finger or a fork to press the half circle closed.

5. Spray the steamer tray with cooking spray. Insert steamer tray into the Copper Chef. Pour in 2 cups of water. Place the pan on high heat.

6. Place the pierogies onto the steamer tray. Be careful they don't overlap too much (so they don't stick together). You may need to do this in batches. Cover and steam for about 4-5 minutes. Set pierogies aside as they are finished.

7. Discard the steaming water. Carefully remove the steamer tray (it will be hot).

8. Add the butter, onion, salt, and black pepper to the pan. Sauté until the onions are golden. Add the pierogies to the butter and onion. Cook until each side is golden.

9. Serve with a spoonful of sour cream and some chives.

Ingredients

3 tbsp. olive oil

1 lb. lean ground beef

salt and pepper

1 onion, chopped fine

2 tbsp. tomato paste

1 tsp. oregano

1 tsp. onion

2 cloves garlic, chopped

1/2 tsp. cinnamon

1/2 cup feta cheese

1/8 cup fresh mint, chopped

1 (12 oz.) pack wonton wrappers

2 cups water

Sauce:

1 cup greek yogurt

1 medium cucumber, seeded and finely chopped

juice of 1/2 lemon

zest of whole lemon

1/8 tsp. dried dill

1/8 cup fresh mint

1/2 tsp. salt

1/2 tsp. pepper

Greek Wonton Pot Stickers

Directions

1. For the sauce: blend all ingredients thoroughly in a blender.

2. For the filling: put the Copper Chef on medium-high heat. When the pan is hot, add olive oil. Brown the ground beef for about 5 minutes. Drain excess fat.

3. Add onion, tomato paste, oregano, garlic, and cinnamon. Cook for 2 minutes.

4. Turn the heat down to low. Stir in the feta cheese and mint. Cover and cook for 2 minutes.

5. Remove the lid. Stir to incorporate feta until there are no lumps. Transfer to a bowl. Let cool for about 5 minutes.

6. On a flat surface, one wonton wrapper at a time, dip your finger into clean water. Lightly wet the edges of the wonton. Fill with 1/2 tsp. of the ground beef mixture. Fold into a triangle. Press the edges closed with your finger or a fork.

7. When the wontons are finished, place the steamer tray into the Copper Chef. Add 2 cups of water and bring water to a boil.

8. Place wontons (in batches) onto the steamer tray. Cover. Steam each batch until done, about 20 minutes per batch.

Eric's Tip: These pot stickers are also delicious deep-fried. Simply follow the recipe until you get to the steam direction. Fill the Copper Chef with 2 quarts of oil and heat to 365° F. Cook until golden brown.

Chicken and Scallion Pot Stickers

Ingredients

2 chicken breasts, cooked and trimmed

4 scallions, chopped

2 tbsp. water chestnuts, chopped

2 cloves garlic

1 tbsp. ginger

½ tsp. sea salt

¼ tsp. ground black pepper

2 egg whites, beaten

20 wonton wrappers

2 tbsp. canola oil

2 cups water

Dipping Sauce

¼ cup rice vinegar

1 tbsp. soy sauce

1 tbsp. sugar

1 tbsp. sweet chili sauce

¼ tsp. sesame oil

1 pinch sesame seeds

Directions

1. Reserve: ingredients for dipping sauce, wonton wrappers, egg whites, and canola oil. Chop the rest of the ingredients in a food processor.

2. Place a wonton wrapper on the counter. Place 1 tbsp. of the chicken filling in the middle of the wonton. Brush the outer edges with beaten egg whites and seal. Repeat with the rest of the wonton wrappers.

3. Place the Copper Chef on medium heat. Pour in about 2 inches of water. Oil the steamer tray, then place it into the Copper Chef.

4. Place pot stickers on the tray. Place the lid on the pan and steam until tender (about 7-10 minutes). Remove pot stickers and set aside.

5. Dry the Copper Chef, then place canola oil on medium heat. Lightly brown both sides of the pot stickers.

6. Make the dipping sauce: mix all the sauce ingredients in a bowl.

7. Serve pot stickers with dipping sauce.

Eric's Tip: The beauty of this recipe is that you can use absolutely anything for the filling. Meat, fish, seafood, vegetables, etc. You can even use your leftovers from last night's dinner! Just make sure not to overfill the wonton wrappers.

SERVES 6

Ingredients

¾ cup white wine

2 cups water

2 bay leaves

6 flounder fillets

1 tsp. sea salt

1 tsp. ground black pepper

Pesto:

3 cups fresh basil, leaves

½ cup parsley

¼ cup pine nuts

⅓ cup olive oil

½ tsp. sea salt

½ tsp. ground black pepper

¼ cup Parmesan cheese

Pesto-Stuffed Flounder

Directions

1. Pour the white wine, water, and bay leaves in the Copper Chef. Insert the steamer tray. Cover and turn to medium heat.

2. Blend all the pesto ingredients in a blender or food processor.

3. Lay the fillets out on a cutting board. Season with sea salt and black pepper. Spoon some pesto onto each fillet and roll. Place the rolled fillets onto the steamer tray.

4. Cover. Increase heat to medium-high. Cook for about 6-8 minutes or until done.

5. Serve.

New England Clam Bake

SERVES 6

Ingredients

4 tbsp. butter

2 shallots, peeled and sliced

8 oz. chorizo, sliced

6 baby potatoes, cut in half

1 dozen clams

1 dozen mussels

2 ears corn, cut in 3 sections

2 Roma tomatoes, diced

1 bottle of beer

juice of 1 lemon

1 bay leaf

1 lemon, quartered

1 cup water

2 tbsp. lemon zest

4 parsley stems

Directions

1. Place the Copper Chef on medium-high heat. Melt the butter. Sweat the shallots for 2 minutes.

2. Add the chorizo and potatoes. Cook on medium-high for about 5 minutes, stirring occasionally, until the potatoes are cooked firm.

3. Turn the heat to high. Add the rest of the ingredients. Cover. Cook until the clams and mussels open. Serve immediately.

4. Be sure to discard any clam or mussel that does not open.

Eric's Tip: If you take all of the contents out of the pan and leave just the liquid, you can then reduce the liquid by about one third. That will give you a much more concentrated broth. Pour this broth over the clams and mussels. Serve immediately.

Halibut with Dijon and Tomato Drizzle

Ingredients

4 (6-8 oz.) halibut fillets

juice of half of a lemon

1 tsp. dried thyme

salt and pepper

2 cups water

Dressing:

2 tbsp. spicy brown mustard

1 tbsp. honey

3 tbsp. mayonnaise

2 tbsp. tomato paste

1 tsp soy sauce

juice of half of a lemon

salt and pepper

Directions

1. In a mixing bowl, combine all of the dressing ingredients. Whisk well until combined.

2. Place the steamer tray in the Copper Chef. Add 3 cups of water. Turn the heat to high.

3. Rub the lemon juice on all of the halibut fillets. Season equally with salt, pepper, and thyme.

4. Using tongs, place the halibut onto the steamer tray. Cover with the lid.

5. Lower the heat to medium-high. Keep covered and steam for about 15 minutes. Check periodically to make sure the water hasn't boiled dry. If water gets low, just add more.

6. Place the fish onto a platter. Drizzle the dressing onto each filet. Add salt and pepper, to taste.

7. Serve immediately over a bed of greens.

Herb-Steamed Shrimp

Ingredients

2 tbsp. olive oil

1 tbsp. butter

3 cloves garlic, crushed

½ cup parsley, chopped

½ cup cilantro, chopped

juice of 2 limes

salt and pepper

½ tsp. seafood seasoning

2 cups white wine

2 sprigs fresh thyme

12 shrimp, large, peeled and deveined

Directions

1. Place the Copper Chef on medium-high heat. When the pan is hot, add olive oil and butter. Sauté the garlic, parsley, cilantro, lime juice, salt, pepper, and seafood seasoning for about 3 minutes.

2. Set aside in a small bowl.

3. Add white wine and thyme to the pan. Place on high heat.

4. Place the steamer tray into the Copper Chef. Add all of the shrimp onto the tray.

5. Cover with the lid. Cook on high heat until the shrimp are pink (about 6 minutes).

6. Remove shrimp from the Copper Chef. Toss shrimp into the garlic herb mixture before serving.

Steamed Salmon with Leeks and Asparagus

Ingredients

1 tbsp. olive oil

2 tbsp. butter

1 cup leeks, finely sliced

1 shallot, peeled and minced

1 lemon, juiced

½ tsp. sea salt

½ tsp. ground black pepper

½ tsp. dried thyme

1 cup white wine

1 sprig thyme

1 bay leaf

1 cup water

2 (4oz.) salmon fillets, skinless

12 asparagus stalks, cleaned and trimmed

sea salt and black pepper, to season salmon

Directions

1. Place the Copper Chef on medium-high heat. Once the pan is hot, add the oil and butter. Add the shallots, leeks, lemon juice, dried thyme, sea salt, and black pepper. Sauté until the leeks are tender. Set aside in a small bowl.

2. Add white wine, water, fresh thyme, and bay leaf to the pan.

3. Place the steamer tray into the Copper Chef. Place the salmon and asparagus on top of the tray, side by side.

4. Season the fish with sea salt and black pepper. Top with the leek mixture.

5. Place on high heat and steam for 8-10 minutes or until desired doneness.

6. Serve.

Whole Thai Steamed Snapper

SERVES 4-6

Ingredients

1 (2-3 lb.) snapper, cleaned with head and tail on

2 tbsp. toasted sesame oil

2 cloves garlic, smashed

1 Thai chili, sliced

2 tbsp. soy sauce

1 fresh lime, zest and juice

2 cups water

1 tbsp. brown sugar

3 tbsp. fresh ginger, julienned

¼ cup cilantro leaves

¼ cup fresh basil leaves

1 scallion, 1-inch sliced

Directions

1. Make 4 diagonal slices, 1 inch apart, on both sides of the fish. This helps with even cooking and flavor penetration.

2. In a bowl, combine sesame oil, soy sauce, garlic, chili, brown sugar, 2 tbsp. of the ginger, lime zest and juice.

3. Stuff fish cavity with cilantro, scallion, basil, and squeezed lime halves.

4. Insert the steamer tray into the Copper Chef on medium heat. Add 2 cups water

5. Place fish on the steamer tray. Pour marinade over fish. Cover.

6. Reduce heat to low. Steam for 15-20 minutes, or until fish is cooked through.

Eric's Tip: After you remove the fish from the Copper Chef, bring the steaming liquid to a light simmer and add a little cornstarch slurry to thicken. Strain the sauce and enjoy over jasmine rice.

Herb-Steamed Potatoes

Ingredients

2 large Yukon Gold potatoes, cubed

4 cups water

2 sprigs rosemary

4 sprigs tarragon

4 sprigs thyme

1 tbsp. sea salt

3 tbsp. butter

1 tsp. dry rosemary

½ tsp. ground black pepper

½ tsp. sea salt

2 tbsp. parsley, chopped

Directions

1. In the Copper Chef, add water, rosemary, tarragon, thyme, and sea salt. Insert the steamer tray into the Copper Chef. Place potatoes on top. Cover. Cook until the potatoes are fork-tender.

2. Remove the potatoes and drain the Copper Chef. Melt the butter. Add the potatoes back in with the dried rosemary, black pepper, sea salt, and parsley.

3. Toss to coat the potatoes before serving.

Eric's Tip: For added decadence, add ½ cup heavy cream at the very end when tossing potatoes.

Steamed Snow Crab Legs

Ingredients

3 lb. snow crab legs

3 tbsp. seafood seasoning

1 bay leaf

1 bottle of beer

1 cup water

For the Butter:

1 stick butter

1 tbsp. horseradish, jarred

2 tbsp. lemon juice

½ cup parsley or cilantro, chopped

zest of 1 lemon

salt and pepper, to taste

Directions

1. Place the seafood seasoning, bay leaf, beer, and water into the Copper Chef.

2. Insert the steamer tray into the Copper Chef. Place the snow crab on top.

3. Cover and cook on high heat. Steam the crab for about 7-8 minutes.

4. Using a microwave-safe bowl, combine the butter and horseradish. Microwave until the butter liquefies. Carefully remove the bowl from the microwave and stir in the lemon juice, lemon zest, and fresh herbs. Season with salt and pepper, to taste.

5. Serve the crab legs with the horseradish butter.

Index

t: Eric's tip

p: Recipe Photo

A

alfredo
Chicken Alfredo, 85
pie, 159t
apple cider, 137
Apple Fritters, 53
Apple Slaw, Pan-Seared Pork Chops with, 93
apples
about, 93t
Apple Fritters, 53
Bacon-Wrapped Roast Pork, 77
Pan-Seared Herb Pork Chops with Apple Slaw, 93
Sticky Buns, 178t
Wiener Schnitzel with Braised Red Cabbage, 137
Arborio rice, 84
arugula, 44
asado, 91, 91t
Asian-inspired
Asparagus, Bacon and Spinach, 191
Chicken and Scallion Pot Stickers, 223
Greek Wonton Pot Stickers, 222
Miso-Glazed Salmon, 70
Mongolian Beef, 194
Pepper Steak, 187
Pork Fried Rice, 188
Shrimp and Asparagus, 192
Spicy Asian Beef Wraps, 183
Spring Rolls, 34
Steak and Soba Noodles, 184
Teriyaki Pork Tenderloins, 148
Thai Coconut Chicken Soup, 204
Vegetable Fried Rice, 195
Vegetable Lo Mein, 196
Whole Thai Steamed Snapper, 230
asparagus
Asparagus, Bacon and Spinach, 190p, 191
Shrimp and Asparagus, 192
Steamed Salmon with Leeks and Asparagus, 229
Vegetable Tempura, 26
Au Gratin Potatoes, 156, 157p
Austria-inspired, 137

B

bacon
about, 77t
Asparagus, Bacon and Spinach, 191
Bacon-Wrapped Roast Pork, 77
Coq Au Vin, 123
Linguini Carbonara, 112
New England Clam Chowder, 205
Quiche Lorraine, 149
soup, adding to, 200t
Texas Smokehouse Stuffed Burger, 86
White Bean (soup), 201

baked. *See also* **desserts**
Au Gratin Potatoes, 156
Baked Ziti, 161
Beef Enchiladas, 141
Bleu Cheese Stuffed Mushrooms, 153
Chicken Parm, 142
Chicken Pot Pie, 143
Cornbread, 174
Eggplant Parmesan, 155
Giant Frittata, 150
Lime Cilantro Seafood Bake, 154
Noodle Kugel, 162
Pineapple-Glazed Ham, 147
Quiche Lorraine, 149
Sausage Frittata, 144
Shepherd's Pie, 140
Spaghetti Pie, 159
Stuffed Pork Medallions, 145
Sweet Potatoes with Marshmallows, 160
Teriyaki Pork Tenderloins, 148
Vegetable Lasagna, 163
Baked Ziti, 161
Baklava, 175
balsamic glaze, 215t
Banana Nut Bread, 177
Bang Bang Chicken, 30, 31p
barley, 212
BBQ Baby Back Ribs, 72p, 73
BBQ sauce, 86. *See also* **asado**
beans
about, 110t
Cuban Pork Asado with Black Bean Relish, 91
Eric's Beef Chili, 209
Super Easy Turkey Chili, 217
White Bean (soup), 201
beef, ground. *See also* **beef**
Beef Enchiladas, 141
Eric's Beef Chili, 209
Greek Wonton Pot Stickers, 222
Meatballs and Sunday Gravy, 118
Mom's Meatloaf, 58
Shepherd's Pie, 140
Spaghetti Pie, 159
Spicy Asian Beef Wraps, 183
Swedish Meatballs, 121
Texas Smokehouse Stuffed Burger, 86
beef. *See also* **beef, ground**
about, 184t
Beef Stew, 131
Classic Beef Barley, 212
Country Fried Steak, 41
Mongolian Beef, 194
Pepper Steak, 187
Philly Cheesesteak, 82
Roast Beef, 65
Roast Prime Rib of Beef, 61
Spicy Cowboy Steak, 62
Steak and Soba Noodles, 184, 185p
Veal and Peppers, 122
Wiener Schnitzel with Braised Red Cabbage, 137
beer

Beef Stew, 131
Eric's French Quarter Chili, 215
Lamb Stew, 136
New England Clam Bake, 225
Bisque, Shrimp, 208
Black Bean Relish, Cuban Pork Asado with, 91
Black Forest Cake, 169
black-eyed peas, 215
Bleu Cheese Stuffed Mushrooms, 152p, 153
Blueberry Breakfast Cake with Crumb Topping, 166, 167p
bok choy, baby
Steak and Soba Noodles, 184
Vegetable Fried Rice, 195
Bouillabaisse, Seafood, 210
Boursin cheese, 61t
Braciole, Pork, 132p, 133
braised
about, 117
Braised Lamb Shanks, 134, 135p
Braised Pork Shoulder, 130
Braised Pork Shoulder with Browned Sauerkraut, 127
Chicken and Dumplings, 125
Chicken Cacciatore, 124
and Copper Chef, 117
Coq Au Vin, 123
Green Chile Pork, 126
Lamb Stew, 136
Meatballs and Sunday Gravy, 118
Pork Braciole, 133
Pork Osso Buco, 129
Swedish Meatballs, 121
Veal and Peppers, 122
brandy, 208
breadcrumbs, 58t
breads
Banana Nut Bread, 177
Blueberry Breakfast Cake with Crumb Topping, 166
Coffee Cake, 168
Cornbread, 174
Glazed Doughnuts, 51
Pumpkin Doughnuts, 52
Sticky Buns, 178
breakfasts
Apple Fritters, 53
Banana Nut Bread, 177
Blueberry Breakfast Cake with Crumb Topping, 166
burrito, 141t
Coffee Cake, 168
French toast, 176t
Giant Frittata, 150
Glazed Doughnuts, 51
Pumpkin Doughnuts, 52
Quiche Lorraine, 149
Sausage Frittata, 144
Sticky Buns, 178
Brick Chicken, Spicy, 67
brine
about, 69t
Orange Brine Turkey Breast, 69

Roasted Pork Loin, 75
broth, 225t
Brown Butter, Roasted Cauliflower Soup with, 203
Browned Sauerkraut, Braised Pork Shoulder with, 127
brownies
Cheesecake Brownies, 179
Fried Brownies, 50
Peanut Butter Brownies, 172, 173p
brunch, 154t. *See also* **breakfasts**
Buns, Sticky, 178
Burger, Texas Smokehouse Stuffed, 86, 87p
Burgers, Salmon, 108
burrito, 141t, 187t
butter, 233

C
cabbage
Braised Pork Shoulder with Browned Sauerkraut, 127
Pan-Seared Herb Pork Chops with Apple Slaw, 93
Pork Fried Rice, 188
Spring Rolls, 34
Wiener Schnitzel with Braised Red Cabbage, 137
Cacciatore, Chicken, 124
Cajun-inspired, 215
cake
Black Forest Cake, 169
Blueberry Breakfast Cake with Crumb Topping, 166
Coconut Cake, 171
Coffee Cake, 168
Pumpkin Cake, 176
cake mix, 171, 171t
caramel sauce, 171t
Carbonara, Linguini, 112, 113p
Caribbean Jerk Chicken Wings, 38
carrots
Beef Stew, 131
Braised Lamb Shanks, 134
Braised Pork Shoulder, 130
Braised Pork Shoulder with Browned Sauerkraut, 127
Chicken Pot Pie, 143
Classic Beef Barley, 212
Coq Au Vin, 123
Flounder in Saffron Tomato Broth, 109
Lamb Stew, 136
Meatballs and Sunday Gravy, 118
Mom's Meatloaf, 58
Orange Brine Turkey Breast, 69
Pork Fried Rice, 188
Pork Osso Buco, 129
Shepherd's Pie, 140
Shrimp Bisque, 208
Shrimp Gumbo, 207
Split Pea (soup), 202
Spring Rolls, 34
Steak and Soba Noodles, 184
Stuffed Pork Medallions, 145

Pesto-Stuffed Flounder, 224
French toast, 176t
French-inspired
   Au Gratin Potatoes, 156
   Coq Au Vin, 123
   Seafood Bouillabaisse, 210
   Shrimp Bisque, 208
   Tilapia Francese, 104
fried, deep. *See* **deep-fried**
Fried Brownies, 50
Fried Chicken, 16p, 42p, 43
Fried Chocolate Cream-Filled Cookies, 48, 49p
fried rice
   Pork Fried Rice, 188, 188p
   Vegetable Fried Rice, 195
Fried Zucchini Sticks, 19
fries
   Garlic Truffle Fries, 22
   Sweet Potato Fries, 21
frittatas
   Giant Frittata, 150, 151p
   Sausage Frittata, 144
fritters
   Apple Fritters, 53
   Corn Fritters, 25
frosting
   coconut, 171
   Glazed Doughnuts, 51
fruits, in cakes, 166t
Fusilli and Clams, 111

G

garlic
   Garlic Truffle Fries, 22, 23p
   Parmesan Garlic Wings, 39
German-inspired
   Black Forest Cake, 169
   Wiener Schnitzel with Braised Red Cabbage, 137t
Giant Frittata, 150, 151p
ginger ale, 26t
Glazed Doughnuts, 46p, 51
Glazed Ham, Pineapple, 146p, 147
goat cheese, 90t
gravy
   Country Fried Steak, 41
   Meatballs and Sunday Gravy, 118
   Orange Brine Turkey Breast, 69
Greek Wonton Pot Stickers, 222
Greek-inspired, 175, 222
Green Chile Pork, 126
Greens, Pan-Seared Scallops Over, 100, 101p
ground beef. *See* **beef, ground**
Guinness beer, 136
Gumbo, Shrimp, 206p, 207

H

half and half, 149t
Halibut with Dijon and Tomato Drizzle, 226p, 227
ham
   Giant Frittata, 150
   Monte Cristo Americano, 40
   Pineapple-glazed Ham, 147
   Split Pea (soup), 202
hamburger. *See* **beef, ground**
hashbrowns
   about, 144t
   Giant Frittata, 150
heavy cream, 149t
herb rub, 69
Herb-Steamed Potatoes, 232
Herb-Steamed Shrimp, 228
Hollandaise sauce, 22t
hominy, 214
honey maple mustard, 21t
hors d'oeuvre, 29t
horseradish, 19, 65
Hot and Sweet Sausage and Peppers, 102p, 103
hot sauce
   Bang Bang Chicken, 30
   Fried Chicken, 43t
Hungarian-inspired, 88

I

ice cream, 50p
icing, 51
Italian-inspired
   Chicken Cacciatore, 124
   Chicken Parm, 142
   Eggplant Parmesan, 155
   Giant Frittata, 150
   Linguini Carbonara, 112
   Pork Braciole, 133
   Pork Osso Buco, 129
   Sausage Frittata, 144
   Shrimp and Saffron Risotto, 84
   Zeppole, 55

J

Jamaican-inspired, 74
Jerk Ribs, 74
jerk sauce, 38, 38t
Jewish-inspired, 162

K

Kugel, Noodle, 162

L

lamb
Braised Lamb Shanks, 134, 135p
cooking, 78t
Lamb Stew, 136
Rosemary Rack of Lamb, 78
Lasagna, Vegetable, 163
Leeks and Asparagus, Steamed Salmon with, 229
lettuce wraps
Bang Bang Chicken as, 30t
Spicy Asian Beef Wraps, 183
Lime Cilantro Seafood Bake, 154
Linguini Carbonara, 112, 113p
liquor. *See individual types*
Lo Mein, Vegetable, 196, 197p
Loaded Baked Potato Gratin, 156t
lobster tails, 210

M

Mango Pineapple Salsa, Pan-Seared Tuna with, 106, 107p
maple syrup, 160
marinade
Miso-Glazed Salmon, 70
Mongolian Beef, 194
Marinara sauce, 133
Marshmallows, Sweet Potatoes with, 160
Maryland, taste of, 99t
meat. *See individual* **types; stir-fry**
meatballs
about, 118t
Baked Ziti, 161
Meatballs and Sunday Gravy, 118, 119p
Swedish Meatballs, 120p, 121
Meatloaf, Mom's, 58, 59p
Medallions, Stuffed Pork, 145
Mexican-inspired
Beef Enchiladas, 141
Pozole Guerrero, 214
Tortilla Soup, 213
Middle Eastern-inspired, 175
mint, 134t
Miso-Glazed Salmon, 70, 71p
Mom's Meatloaf, 58, 59p
Mongolian Beef, 194
Monte Cristo Americano, 40
mozzarella cheese
Baked Ziti, 161
Chicken Parm, 142

Eggplant Parmesan, 155
Spaghetti Pie, 159
Vegetable Lasagna, 163
mushrooms
about, 98t, 124t
Bleu Cheese Stuffed Mushrooms, 153
Chicken Breasts with Tomato Tapenade, 90
Chicken Cacciatore, 124
Classic Beef Barley, 212
Coq Au Vin, 123
Cream of Mushroom, 200
Pork Marsala with Mushrooms and Spinach, 98
Spicy Asian Beef Wraps, 183
Spring Rolls, 34
Stuffed Pork Medallions, 145
Vegetable Fried Rice, 195
Vegetable Lasagna, 163
Vegetable Lo Mein, 196
Vegetable Tempura, 26
mussels
New England Clam Bake, 225
Seafood Bouillabaisse, 210
Spicy Mussels, 94p, 95

N

New England Clam Bake, 225
New England Clam Chowder, 205
Noodle Kugel, 162
noodle pudding, 162
noodles. *See also* **pasta**
Lo Mein, 196
soba, 184
Nut Bread, Banana, 177
nuts
Baklava, 175
Banana Nut Bread, 177
Chicken Breasts with Tomato Tapenade, 90
Pork Braciole, 133
Sticky Buns, 178
substitute for, 177t

O

okra, 207
olives, 90
onions
Cheese and Onion Pierogies, 220
Onion Rings, 18
Orange Brine Turkey Breast, 68p, 69
oranges, 69
Osso Buco, Pork, 129
oven-roasting. *See* **roasting, oven**

P

Pan-Seared Herb Pork Chops with Apple Slaw, 92p, 93

Pan-Seared Scallops Over Greens, 100, 101p

Pan-Seared Tuna with Mango Pineapple Salsa, 106, 107p

paprika, 88

Paprikash, Chicken, 88

Parm, Chicken, 142

Parmesan cheese
  Au Gratin Potatoes, 156
  Baked Ziti, 161
  Chicken Parm, 142
  Eggplant Parmesan, 155
  Linguini Carbonara, 112
  Parmesan Garlic Wings, 39
  Pork Braciole, 133
  Spaghetti Pie, 159
  Vegetable Lasagna, 163

Parmigiano Reggiano, 84, 85

parsnips, 212

pasta
  Baked Ziti, 161
  Chicken Alfredo, 85
  Fusilli and Clams, 111
  Linguini Carbonara, 112
  Penne alla Vodka, 115
  Spaghetti Pie, 159

Peanut Butter Brownies, 172, 173p

pears, 93t

peas
  Chicken Pot Pie, 143
  Eric's French Quarter Chili, 215
  Lamb Stew, 136
  Pork Fried Rice, 188
  Shepherd's Pie, 140
  Split Pea (soup), 202
  Vegetable Fried Rice, 195
  Vegetable Lo Mein, 196

Penne alla Vodka, 114p, 115

peppers
  about, 74t
  Bleu Cheese Stuffed Mushrooms, 153
  Caribbean Jerk Chicken Wings, 38
  Chicken Cacciatore, 124
  Corn Fritters, 25, 25t
  Cornbread, 174
  Eric's Beef Chili, 209
  Eric's French Quarter Chili, 215
  Green Chile Pork, 126
  Hot and Sweet Sausage and Peppers, 103
  Lime Cilantro Seafood Bake, 154
  New England Clam Chowder, 205
  Pan-Seared Tuna with Mango Pineapple Salsa, 106
  Pan-Seared Tuna with Mango Pineapple Sauce, 106
  Pepper Steak, 186p, 187
  Philly Cheesesteak, 82
  Pozole Guerrero, 214
  Sausage Frittata, 144
  Shrimp Gumbo, 207

Steak and Soba Noodles, 184
  Stuffed Pork Medallions, 145
  Super Easy Turkey Chili, 217
  Thai Coconut Chicken Soup, 204
  Tortilla Soup, 213
  Veal and Peppers, 122
  Vegetable Fried Rice, 195
  Vegetable Lasagna, 163
  Vegetable Lo Mein, 196

Pesto-Stuffed Flounder, 224

Philly Cheesesteak, 82, 83p

pie
  Chicken Pot Pie, 143
  crust, 143t
  Quiche Lorraine, 149
  Spaghetti Pie, 159

Pierogies, Cheese and Onion, 220, 220p

pineapple
  Pan-Seared Tuna with Mango Pineapple Salsa, 106
  Pineapple-Glazed Ham, 146p, 147

Po' Boy Sandwich, 41t

Polish-inspired, 220

pork
  about, 129t
  Bacon-Wrapped Roast Pork, 77
  Braised Pork Shoulder, 130
  Braised Pork Shoulder with Browned Sauerkraut, 127
  chops, 62t
  Cuban Pork Asado with Black Bean Relish, 91
  dried, 112t
  Eric's French Quarter Chili, 215
  Green Chile Pork, 126
  loin, 65t
  Meatballs and Sunday Gravy, 118
  Mom's Meatloaf, 58
  Pan-Seared Herb Pork Chops with Apple Slaw, 93
  Pork Braciole, 132p, 133
  Pork Fried Rice, 188, 188p
  Pork Marsala with Mushrooms and Spinach, 98
  Pork Osso Buco, 128p, 129
  Pozole Guerrero, 214
  Prosciutto-Wrapped Cod with Edamame Salad, 110
  Roasted Pork Loin, 75
  shanks, 134t
  Stuffed Pork Medallions, 145
  substitute for, 214t
  Teriyaki Pork Tenderloins, 148

pot stickers
  Chicken and Scallion Pot Stickers, 223
  filling, 223t
  frying, 222t
  Greek Wonton Pot Stickers, 222

potatoes. *See also* **sweet potatoes; yams**
  about, 130t
  Au Gratin Potatoes, 156, 157p
  Beef Stew, 131
  Cheese and Onion Pierogies, 220
  Chicken Alfredo, 85t
  Chicken Pot Pie, 143
  flakes, 208
  Garlic Truffle Fries, 22

Giant Frittata, 150
Herb-Steamed Potatoes, 232
Lamb Stew, 136
Lime Cilantro Seafood Bake, 154
New England Clam Bake, 225
New England Clam Chowder, 205
Sausage Frittata, 144
Pot Pie, Chicken, 143
poultry sausage, 103t
Poutine, 19t
Pozole Guerrero, 214
proofing, 51t
Prosciutto-Wrapped Cod with Edamame Salad, 110
provolone cheese, 82
pudding, 55t
pudding, noodle, 162
pumpkin
Pumpkin Cake, 176
Pumpkin Doughnuts, 52

Q
Quiche Lorraine, 149

R
Rack of Lamb, Rosemary, 78, 79p
raisins, 133
ranch dressing, 36t
Red Cabbage, Braised with Wiener Schnitzel, 137
red pepper flakes, 191t
relish, 91
ribs
BBQ Baby Back Ribs, 72p, 73
boiling, 73t
Jerk Ribs, 74
rice
Pork Fried Rice, 188
Shrimp and Saffron Risotto, 84
Vegetable Fried Rice, 195
ricotta cheese
Baked Ziti, 161
Cheese and Onion Pierogies, 220
Spaghetti Pie, 159
Vegetable Lasagna, 163
risotto
about, 84t
Shrimp and Saffron Risotto, 84
Roast Beef, 64p, 65
Roast Pork, Bacon-Wrapped, 76p, 77
Roast Prime Rib of Beef, 60p, 61
Roasted Cauliflower Soup with Brown Butter, 203
Roasted Chicken, Classic, 66

Roasted Pork Loin, 75
roasting, oven
Bacon-Wrapped Roast Pork, 77
BBQ Baby Back Ribs, 73
Classic Roasted Chicken, 66
and Copper Chef, 57
Jerk Ribs, 74
Miso-Glazed Salmon, 70
Mom's Meatloaf, 58
Orange Brine Turkey Breast, 69
Roast Beef, 65
Roast Prime Rib of Beef, 61
Roasted Pork Loin, 75
Rosemary Rack of Lamb, 78
Spicy Brick Chicken, 67
Spicy Cowboy Steak, 62
Roquefort cheese, 61t
Rosemary Rack of Lamb, 78, 79p
rubs
BBQ Baby Back Ribs, 73
jerk seasoning, 74
Orange Brine Turkey Breast, 69

S
saffron
Flounder in Saffron Tomato Broth, 109
Seafood Bouillabaisse, 210
Shrimp and Saffron Risotto, 84
substitute for, 210t
salads
about, 100t
Chicken Milanese with Arugula and Fennel Salad, 44
Pan-Seared Scallops Over Greens, 100
Prosciutto-Wrapped Cod with Edamame Salad, 110
salmon
Lime Cilantro Seafood Bake, 154
Miso-Glazed Salmon, 70
Salmon Burgers, 108
Steamed Salmon with Leeks and Asparagus, 229
salsa
Beef Enchiladas, 141
mango pineapple, 106
ranch dip, 21t
salsa verde
Pozole Guerrero, 214
Super Easy Turkey Chili, 217
sandwiches
and meatballs, 121t
Monte Cristo Americano, 40
Philly Cheesesteak, 82
Po' Boy, 41t
and Pork Braciole, 133t
Texas Smokehouse Stuffed Burger, 86
sauces. *See also* **dipping sauce**
Bacon-Wrapped Roast Pork, 77
Bang Bang Chicken, 30
BBQ, 73, 73t, 86
caramel, 171t

Greek Wonton Pot Stickers, 222
Hollandaise, 22t
jerk, 38
Mongolian Beef, 194
Spring Rolls, 34
Stuffed Pork Medallions, 145
Swedish Meatballs, 121
thickening, 230t

sauerkraut, 127

sausage
Eric's French Quarter Chili, 215
Hot and Sweet Sausage and Peppers, 103
New England Clam Bake, 225
Sausage Frittata, 144

sautéed
about, 81
Chicken Alfredo, 85
Chicken Breasts with Tomato Tapenade, 90
Chicken Paprikash, 88
and Copper Chef, 81
Crab Cakes, 99
Cuban Pork Asado with Black Bean Relish, 91
Flounder in Saffron Tomato Broth, 109
Fusilli and Clams, 111
Hot and Sweet Sausage and Peppers, 103
Linguini Carbonara, 112
Pan-Seared Herb Pork Chops with Apple Slaw, 93
Pan-Seared Scallops Over Greens, 100
Pan-Seared Tuna with Mango Pineapple Salsa, 106
Penne alla Vodka, 115
Philly Cheesesteak, 82
Pork Marsala with Mushrooms and Spinach, 98
Prosciutto-Wrapped Cod with Edamame Salad, 110
Salmon Burgers, 108
Shrimp and Saffron Risotto, 84
Spicy Mussels, 95
Summer Clams, 96
Texas Smokehouse Stuffed Burger, 86
Tilapia Francese, 104

savory. *See* **baked**

scallops, sea
about, 100t
as hor d'oeuvre, 29t
Lime Cilantro Seafood Bake, 154
Pan-Seared Scallops Over Greens, 100

Schwarzwälder Kirschtorte, 169

scotch bonnets, 38

seafood
about, 96t
Coconut Shrimp, 29
Crab Cakes, 99
Flounder in Saffron Tomato Broth, 109
Fusilli and Clams, 111
Halibut with Dijon and Tomato Drizzle, 227
Herb-Steamed Shrimp, 228
Lime Cilantro Seafood Bake, 154
Miso-Glazed Salmon, 70
New England Clam Bake, 225
New England Clam Chowder, 205
Pan-Seared Scallops Over Greens, 100
Pan-Seared Tuna with Mango Pineapple Salsa, 106
Pesto-Stuffed Flounder, 224

Prosciutto-Wrapped Cod with Edamame Salad, 110
Salmon Burgers, 108
sea scallops, 29t
Seafood Bouillabaisse, 210, 211p
Shrimp and Asparagus, 192
Shrimp and Saffron Risotto, 84
Shrimp Bisque, 208
Shrimp Gumbo, 207
Spicy Mussels, 95
Steamed Salmon with Leeks and Asparagus, 229
Steamed Snow Crab Legs, 233
substitutions for, 95t
Summer Clams, 96
Tilapia Francese, 104
Whole Thai Steamed Snapper, 230

searing, 194t

sesame seeds, 195t

Sexy Fries, 22t

shellfish. *See* **seafood**

Shepherd's Pie, 140

sherry, 124t

shrimp
Coconut Shrimp, 29
Herb-Steamed Shrimp, 228
Seafood Bouillabaisse, 210
Shrimp and Asparagus, 192, 193p
Shrimp and Saffron Risotto, 84
Shrimp Bisque, 208
Shrimp Gumbo, 206p, 207

Snapper, Whole Thai Steamed, 230, 231p

Snow Crab Legs, Steamed, 218p, 233

Soba Noodles, and Steak, 184, 184p

soups. *See also* **chilies; stew**
and Copper Chef, 199
Cream of Mushroom, 200
New England Clam Chowder, 205
Pozole Guerrero, 214
Roasted Cauliflower Soup with Brown Butter, 203
Shrimp Bisque, 208
Split Pea (soup), 202
Thai Coconut Chicken Soup, 204
Tortilla Soup, 213
White Bean, 201

sour cream, 88

soybeans. See edamame

spaetzle, 137t

Spaghetti Pie, 158p, 159

Spatchcocking, 67t

speck, 112t

spices, 74t

spices, adding, 191t

Spicy Asian Beef Wraps, 182p, 183

Spicy Brick Chicken, 67

Spicy Cowboy Steak, 62, 63p

Spicy Mussels, 94p, 95

spinach
Asparagus, Bacon and Spinach, 191
Chicken Breasts with Tomato Tapenade, 90t
Pork Braciole, 133

Pork Marsala with Mushrooms and Spinach, 98
Vegetable Lasagna, 163
Vegetable Lo Mein, 196
Split Pea (soup), 202
Spring Rolls, 34, 35p
squash, ycllow, 163
Sriracha ketchup, 21t
steamed
about, 219
Cheese and Onion Pierogies, 220
Chicken and Scallion Pot Stickers, 223
Greek Wonton Pot Stickers, 222
Halibut with Dijon and Tomato Drizzle, 227
Herb-Steamed Potatoes, 232
Herb-Steamed Shrimp, 228
New England Clam Bake, 225
Pesto-Stuffed Flounder, 224
Steamed Salmon with Leeks and Asparagus, 229
Steamed Snow Crab Legs, 233
Whole Thai Steamed Snapper, 230
steaming rack, 57
stew
Beef Stew, 131
Classic Beef Barley, 212
Lamb Stew, 136
Pozole Guerrero, 214
Seafood Bouillabaisse, 210
Shrimp Gumbo, 207
Sticky Buns, 178
stir-fry
Asparagus, Bacon and Spinach, 191
and Copper Chef, 181
Mongolian Beef, 194
Pepper Steak, 187
Pork Fried Rice, 188
Shrimp and Asparagus, 192
Spicy Asian Beef Wraps, 183
Steak and Soba Noodles, 184
Vegetable Fried Rice, 195
Vegetable Lo Mein, 196
Stuffed Pork Medallions, 145
Summer Clams, 96, 97p
Sunday Gravy, Meatballs and, 118
Super Easy Turkey Chili, 216p, 217
Swedish Meatballs, 120p, 121
Sweet Chili Glazed Chicken Wings, 36, 37p
sweet potatoes. *See also* **potatoes**
Flounder in Saffron Tomato Broth, 109
Sweet Potato Fries, 20p, 21
Sweet Potatoes with Marshmallows, 160
Vegetable Tempura, 26
Swiss Cheese
Au Gratin Potatoes, 156
Monte Cristo Americano, 40
Quiche Lorraine, 149
syrup, Baklava, 175

T
tacos, street, 33t
tapenade, 90
Tempura, Vegetable, 26
Tenders, Chicken, 33
Teriyaki Pork Tenderloins, 148
Texas Smokehouse Stuffed Burger, 86, 87p
Thai Coconut Chicken Soup, 204
tilapia
about, 104t
Tilapia Francese, 104
tomatillos
about, 126t
Green Chile Pork, 126
Pozole Guerrero, 214
Super Easy Turkey Chili, 217
tomato sauce
Baked Ziti, 161
Eggplant Parmesan, 155
Vegetable Lasagna, 163
tomatoes
Chicken Breasts with Tomato Tapenade, 90
Chicken Cacciatore, 124
Chicken Paprikash, 88
Cuban Pork Asado with Black Bean Relish, 91
Eric's Beef Chili, 209
Eric's French Quarter Chili, 215
Flounder in Saffron Tomato Broth, 109
Meatballs and Sunday Gravy, 118
New England Clam Bake, 225
Penne alla Vodka, 115
Sausage Frittata, 144
Seafood Bouillabaisse, 210
Shrimp Bisque, 208
Shrimp Gumbo, 207
Spicy Mussels, 95
Super Easy Turkey Chili, 217
Tortilla Soup, 213
Veal and Peppers, 122
Tortilla Soup, 213
Truffle Fries, Garlic, 22
tuna steaks
about, 106t
Pan-Seared Tuna with Mango Pineapple Salsa, 106
turkey
Monte Cristo Americano, 40
Orange Brine Turkey Breast, 69
substitute for, 217t
Super Easy Turkey Chili, 216p, 217
turnips, 140

V
veal
about, 129t
Mom's Meatloaf, 58
Veal and Peppers, 122
Wiener Schnitzel with Braised Red Cabbage, 137

Vegetable Fried Rice, 195
Vegetable Lasagna, 163
Vegetable Lo Mein, 196, 196p
Vegetable Tempura, 26, 27p
vegetables. *See individual types*
vodka, 115

W
walnuts
    Baklava, 175
    Banana Nut Bread, 177
    substitutes for, 177t
water chestnuts
    Chicken and Scallion Pot Stickers, 223
    Spicy Asian Beef Wraps, 183
    Spring Rolls, 34
    Vegetable Fried Rice, 195
whipped cream topping, 169
White Bean (soup), 201
Whole Thai Steamed Snapper, 230, 231p
Wiener Schnitzel with Braised Red Cabbage, 137
wine
    about, 115t, 131t
    Braised Lamb Shanks, 134
    Braised Pork Shoulder, 130
    Braised Pork Shoulder with Browned Sauerkraut, 127
    Chicken Cacciatore, 124
    Classic Beef Barley, 212
    Coq Au Vin, 123
    Eric's Beef Chili, 209
    Flounder in Saffron Tomato Broth, 109
    Fusilli and Clams, 111
    Herb-Steamed Shrimp, 228
    Meatballs and Sunday Gravy, 118
    Pesto-Stuffed Flounder, 224
    Pork Braciole, 133
    Pork Marsala with Mushrooms and Spinach, 98
    Pork Osso Buco, 129
    Roast Prime Rib of Beef, 61
    Seafood Bouillabaisse, 210
    Shrimp and Saffron Risotto, 84
    Spicy Mussels, 95
    Steamed Salmon with Leeks and Asparagus, 229
    Stuffed Pork Medallions, 145
    Summer Clams, 96
    Teriyaki Pork Tenderloins, 148
    Tilapia Francese, 104
    Veal and Peppers, 122
wings, chicken
    Caribbean Jerk Chicken Wings, 38
    Parmesan Garlic Wings, 39
    Sweet Chili Glazed Chicken Wings, 36
wok, 181
wonton wrappers
    Cheese and Onion Pierogies, 220
    Chicken and Scallion Pot Stickers, 223
    Greek Wonton Pot Stickers, 222

wraps, 183t

Y
yams, 140
yellow squash, 163
yogurt, 19, 88t

Z
Zeppole, 54p, 55
Ziti, Baked, 161
zucchini
    Fried Zucchini Sticks, 19
    Vegetable Lasagna, 163